Reading Sight Words in Context

Poems, Stories, Games, and Activities to Strengthen Sight Word Recognition and Increase Fluency

by
Kathryn Wheeler

illustrated by
Julie Anderson

Publisher
Key Education Publishing Company, LLC
Minneapolis, Minnesota

www.keyeducationpublishing.com

ꙩꙨ • ꙩꙨ •

CONGRATULATIONS ON YOUR PURCHASE OF A KEY EDUCATION PRODUCT!

The editors at Key Education are former teachers who bring experience, enthusiasm, and quality to each and every product. Thousands of teachers have looked to the staff at Key Education for new and innovative resources to make their work more enjoyable and rewarding. Key Education is committed to developing and publishing educational materials that will assist teachers in building a strong and developmentally appropriate curriculum for young children.

PLAN FOR GREAT TEACHING EXPERIENCES WHEN YOU USE
EDUCATIONAL MATERIALS FROM KEY EDUCATION PUBLISHING COMPANY, LLC

ꙩꙨ • ꙩꙨ •

Credits
Author: Kathryn Wheeler
Publisher: Sherrill B. Flora
Creative Director: Annette Hollister-Papp
Inside Illustrations: Julie Anderson
Editors: Karen Seberg and Claude Chalk
Cover Design: Annette Hollister-Papp
Production: Key Education Staff

Key Education Publishing Company, LLC
Key Education welcomes manuscripts and product ideas from teachers.
For a copy of our submission guidelines, please send a self-addressed, stamped envelope to:

**Key Education Publishing Company, LLC
Acquisitions Department
9601 Newton Avenue South
Minneapolis, Minnesota 55431**

About the Author

Kathryn Wheeler has worked as a teacher, an educational consultant, and an editor in educational publishing. She has published workbooks, stories, and magazine articles for children. Kate was awarded a Michigan Council for the Arts and Cultural Affairs grant for fiction. She has a B.A. degree in English from Hope College. Kate lives in Michigan with her husband, Don.

Standard Book Number: 978-1-602680-21-0
Reading Sight Words in Context
Copyright © 2009 by Key Education Publishing Company, LLC
Minneapolis, Minnesota 55431

ꙩꙨ • ꙩꙨ •

Introduction

Sight words are the basic building blocks on which sentences are created. They are high-frequency words that good readers recognize instantly. But, that recognition doesn't happen instantly—it takes practice. *Reading Sight Words in Context* was created to offer students the chance to see these high-frequency words in the context of engaging poems and stories and then work with the sight words in games and follow-up activities to help build recognition. This is crucial because children who struggle with sight words will struggle harder with overall reading comprehension and fluency.

The 170 sight words presented in *Reading Sight Words in Context* were researched and compiled from the following well-respected word lists: Dolch Sight Word List (Preprimer, Primer, Grade 1, and Grade 2); 100 Most Frequent Words in Books for Beginning Readers by Elena Bodrova, Deborah Leong, and Dmitri Semenov (1998); The Word Bank of High Frequency Writing Words from Rebecca Sitton's Spelling Sourcebook series (Educators Publishing Service); *Dr. Fry's 1000 Instant Words* by Edward Fry, Ph.D. (Teacher Created Resources, 2004); *The American Heritage Word Frequency Book* by John B. Carroll (Houghton Mifflin, 1971); and *A Basic Vocabulary of Elementary School Children* by Henry D. Rinsland (Rinsland Press, 2007).

Table of Contents

Sight Word Check List   Name

Word	❑	❑	❑	Word	❑	❑	❑	Dates			
a	❑	❑	❑	five	❑	❑	❑				
about	❑	❑	❑	fly	❑	❑	❑	mom	❑	❑	❑
after	❑	❑	❑	for	❑	❑	❑	must	❑	❑	❑
again	❑	❑	❑	four	❑	❑	❑	my	❑	❑	❑
all	❑	❑	❑	from	❑	❑	❑	new	❑	❑	❑
am	❑	❑	❑	funny	❑	❑	❑	nine	❑	❑	❑
an	❑	❑	❑	get	❑	❑	❑	no	❑	❑	❑
and	❑	❑	❑	girl	❑	❑	❑	not	❑	❑	❑
any	❑	❑	❑	give	❑	❑	❑	now	❑	❑	❑
are	❑	❑	❑	go	❑	❑	❑	of	❑	❑	❑
as	❑	❑	❑	good	❑	❑	❑	on	❑	❑	❑
ask	❑	❑	❑	got	❑	❑	❑	one	❑	❑	❑
at	❑	❑	❑	green	❑	❑	❑	or	❑	❑	❑
ate	❑	❑	❑	had	❑	❑	❑	orange	❑	❑	❑
away	❑	❑	❑	has	❑	❑	❑	our	❑	❑	❑
ball	❑	❑	❑	have	❑	❑	❑	out	❑	❑	❑
be	❑	❑	❑	he	❑	❑	❑	over	❑	❑	❑
been	❑	❑	❑	help	❑	❑	❑	people	❑	❑	❑
big	❑	❑	❑	her	❑	❑	❑	play	❑	❑	❑
black	❑	❑	❑	here	❑	❑	❑	please	❑	❑	❑
blue	❑	❑	❑	him	❑	❑	❑	pretty	❑	❑	❑
boy	❑	❑	❑	his	❑	❑	❑	purple	❑	❑	❑
brown	❑	❑	❑	house	❑	❑	❑	put	❑	❑	❑
but	❑	❑	❑	how	❑	❑	❑	ran	❑	❑	❑
by	❑	❑	❑	I	❑	❑	❑	red	❑	❑	❑
call	❑	❑	❑	if	❑	❑	❑	ride	❑	❑	❑
came	❑	❑	❑	in	❑	❑	❑	run	❑	❑	❑
can	❑	❑	❑	into	❑	❑	❑	said	❑	❑	❑
cat	❑	❑	❑	is	❑	❑	❑	saw	❑	❑	❑
come	❑	❑	❑	it	❑	❑	❑	say	❑	❑	❑
could	❑	❑	❑	its	❑	❑	❑	school	❑	❑	❑
dad	❑	❑	❑	jump	❑	❑	❑	see	❑	❑	❑
day	❑	❑	❑	just	❑	❑	❑	seven	❑	❑	❑
did	❑	❑	❑	let	❑	❑	❑	she	❑	❑	❑
do	❑	❑	❑	like	❑	❑	❑	six	❑	❑	❑
dog	❑	❑	❑	little	❑	❑	❑	so	❑	❑	❑
down	❑	❑	❑	long	❑	❑	❑	some	❑	❑	❑
each	❑	❑	❑	look	❑	❑	❑	soon	❑	❑	❑
eat	❑	❑	❑	made	❑	❑	❑	stop	❑	❑	❑
eight	❑	❑	❑	make	❑	❑	❑	take	❑	❑	❑
every	❑	❑	❑	many	❑	❑	❑	ten	❑	❑	❑
find	❑	❑	❑	may	❑	❑	❑	than	❑	❑	❑
first	❑	❑	❑	me	❑	❑	❑	thank	❑	❑	❑

Word	❑	❑	❑
that	❑	❑	❑
the	❑	❑	❑
their	❑	❑	❑
them	❑	❑	❑
then	❑	❑	❑
there	❑	❑	❑
these	❑	❑	❑
they	❑	❑	❑
this	❑	❑	❑
three	❑	❑	❑
time	❑	❑	❑
to	❑	❑	❑
too	❑	❑	❑
tree	❑	❑	❑
two	❑	❑	❑
under	❑	❑	❑
up	❑	❑	❑
us	❑	❑	❑
use	❑	❑	❑
very	❑	❑	❑
walk	❑	❑	❑
want	❑	❑	❑
was	❑	❑	❑
water	❑	❑	❑
we	❑	❑	❑
well	❑	❑	❑
went	❑	❑	❑
were	❑	❑	❑
what	❑	❑	❑
when	❑	❑	❑
where	❑	❑	❑
which	❑	❑	❑
white	❑	❑	❑
who	❑	❑	❑
will	❑	❑	❑
with	❑	❑	❑
work	❑	❑	❑
would	❑	❑	❑
yellow	❑	❑	❑
yes	❑	❑	❑
you	❑	❑	❑
your	❑	❑	❑

Standards Correlation for *Reading Sight Words in Context*

This book supports the NCTE/IRA Standards for the English Language Arts and the recommended teaching practices outlined in the NAEYC/IRA position statement Learning to Read and Write: Developmentally Appropriate Practices for Young Children.

NCTE/IRA Standards for the English Language Arts

Each activity in this book supports one or more of the following standards:

1. **Students read many different types of print and nonprint texts for a variety of purposes.** *Reading Sight Words in Context* includes more than 25 reproducible stories and poems that help students learn sight words as they read the texts.

2. **Students read literature from various time periods, cultures, and genres in order to form an understanding of humanity.** Several units in this book contain activities where teachers share thematic literature with their students.

3. **Students use a variety of strategies to build meaning while reading.** The stories and poems in this book, along with accompanying activities, support students in learning essential sight words. Certain activities also build phonemic awareness, phonics, vocabulary, and retelling skills.

4. **Students communicate in spoken, written, and visual form, for a variety of purposes and a variety of audiences.** While doing the activities in this book, students communicate in spoken form in group discussions and retelling activities, in written form by writing letters and words, and in visual form by drawing, coloring, and circling or marking letters or words. Students demonstrate their understanding of sight words by communicating in all these forms.

5. **Students become participating members of a variety of literacy communities.** The group activities and games in *Reading Sight Words in Context* help teachers build a literacy community.

6. **Students use spoken, written, and visual language for their own purposes, such as to learn, for enjoyment, or to share information.** The books and poems in *Reading Sight Words in Context* can be reproduced and sent home with students, helping to build a personal library. The engaging stories and poems motivate students to read independently, while the skill-building activities support students in becoming more effective independent readers and writers.

NAEYC/IRA Position Statement Learning to Read and Write: Developmentally Appropriate Practices for Young Children

Each activity in this book supports one or more of the following recommended teaching practices for Kindergarten and Primary students:

1. **Teachers read to children daily and provide opportunities for students to independently read both fiction and nonfiction texts.** *Reading Sight Words in Context* contains more than 30 engaging stories and poems for students to read.

2. **Teachers provide balanced literacy instruction that incorporates systematic phonics instruction along with meaningful reading and writing activities.** *Reading Sight Words in Context* incorporates phonemic awareness and phonics activities into the learning of sight words through the use of meaningful stories and poems.

3. **Teachers provide opportunities for students to write many different kinds of texts for different purposes.** The activities in *Reading Sight Words in Context* include many opportunities for students to write letters and words to show their understanding of sight words.

4. **Teachers provide opportunities for children to work in small groups.** *Reading Sight Words in Context* includes many small group activities.

5. **Teachers provide challenging instruction that expands children's knowledge of their world and expands vocabulary.** *Reading Sight Words in Context* expands vocabulary by introducing 170 sight words to students. In addition, the thematic nature of the stories and poems builds students' knowledge of many different topics

Poem Title:

Friends

Sight Words Included:

I

me

my

we

you

your

Looking at Sight Words

1. Make copies of the poem (page 8). Ask students to find and circle the following sight words that are featured in this poem: *I, me, my, we, you, your.*

2. Model writing the individual letters as you write each sight word on the board. Then, ask students to practice writing the words.

3. Look for other sight words in the poem: *am, are, like, two.* You can also work with students on these words, or set the poem aside to use again when these words are introduced in later stories and poems. See the Table of Contents on pages 3 and 4 to find in which story or poem each word is featured.

Playing with Sight Words

1. Make large-sized templates of the featured sight words and copy them. Have students do rainbow writing, tracing the letters of the words with their favorite colors.

2. Copy pages 9 and 10 for each student. Have students complete the pages and color the pictures.

3. Make copies of pages 11–13 for each student. Help students color and cut out the stick-puppet shapes and then attach them to sticks. Read the poem out loud or do a choral reading. Students can use their stick puppets to act out the poem.

Follow-Up Activities

1. Have each student bring a favorite toy to class. "Pose" the toys and ask students to draw portraits of their favorite toys. Make frames out of craft sticks or strips of construction paper for the pictures.

2. Discuss with students their favorite things to do. Select five of their favorite activities and vote on them. Make a chart to show the voting results.

Friends

I am me,
And you are you.
We are we,
But also two.
I like my bear,

You like your train.
You like the sun,
I like the rain.
I ride my bike,
You like to run,

But we both like
Lots of fun!
We are we,
But also two
For I am me,
And you are you!

Tic-Tac-Toe

Circle the letters that spell "**you**."

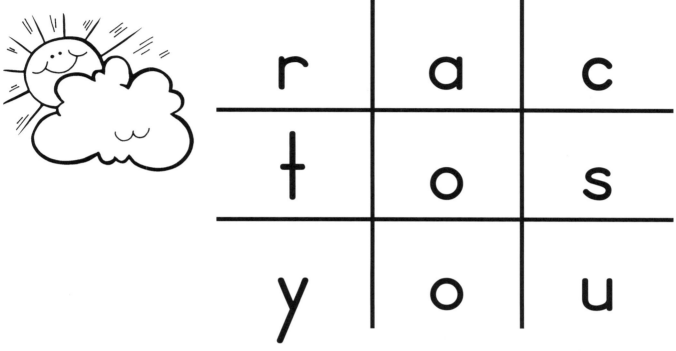

r	a	c
t	o	s
y	o	u

Letter Maze

Circle the letters that spell "**your**."

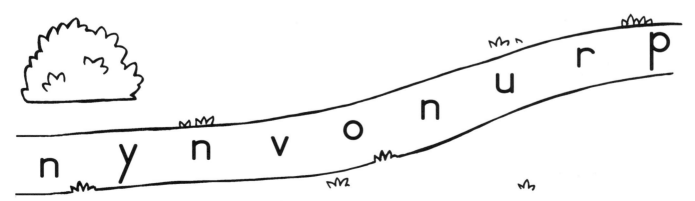

n y n v o n u r p

Name _____

Missing Letters

Fill in the missing letters to write "**me**," "**my**," and "**we**."

Coloring Words

Color all of the flags that have the word "I."

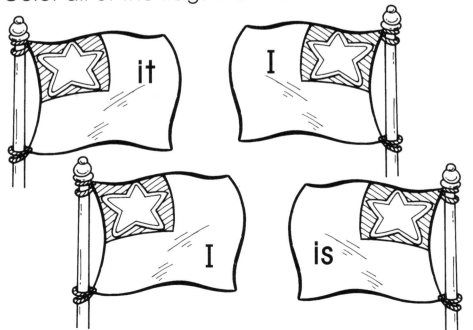
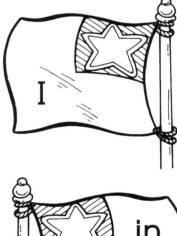

Friends: Stick-Puppet Patterns

Directions: Use the stick-puppet patterns to help tell the story of the poem "Friends" on page 8. Copy, color, and cut out each pattern. Attach each figure to a craft stick with glue or double-sided tape.

OG OG OG OG OG OG OG OG OG OG OG OG OG OG OG OG

Friends: Stick-Puppet Patterns, continued

Friends: Stick-Puppet Patterns, continued

Story Title:

Cat and Dog

⊕G •⊕G •⊕G •⊕G •⊕G •⊕G •⊕G •⊕G •⊕G •⊕G •⊕G •⊕G •⊕G •⊕G •⊕G •⊕G •⊕G •⊕G •⊕G •⊕G •⊕G •⊕G •

Sight Words Included:

a

after

an

away

cat

dog

like

ran

the

Looking at Sight Words

1. Make copies of the story (pages 15–18). Cut each page apart along the dashed line, assemble the story's pages in order, and staple it along the left edge. Ask students to find and circle the following sight words that are featured in this story: *a*, *after*, *an*, *away*, *cat*, *dog*, *like*, *ran*, *the*.

2. Explain to students when *a* is used and when *an* is used. Show them the difference between the words *a cat* and *an ant*. Ask them to help brainstorm oral lists of nouns for each article, for example, *a—dog, store, rock* and *an—elephant, office, arm*, etc.

3. Look for other sight words in the story: *eat, good, he, her, no, one, they, were*. You can also work with students on these words, or set the story aside to use again when these words are introduced in later stories and poems. See the Table of Contents on pages 3 and 4 to find in which story or poem each word is featured.

Playing with Sight Words

1. Make alphabet letter cards to spell each of the featured sight words. Create a set of cards for each group of students. Have students work in teams to assemble the featured sight words with the cards.

2. Copy page 19 for each student. Have students complete the page and color the pictures.

3. Play a word families game. Ask students to stand up when they hear a word that rhymes with the featured sight word. Name a sight word and then give them two or three choices for each word. Examples: *cat, can, mat; dog, log, dawn; like, sight, bike; ran, rain, van; away, stay, awake*; etc.

Follow-Up Activities

1. Study ants! Take students outdoors. Scatter bread crumbs and watch the ants at work.

2. Ask students about cats and dogs as pets. How are they different? Talk about the different things they eat, how they play, what toys they like, and so on.

Cat and Dog

A cat and an ant were friends.
"I like you," said the cat.
"I like you, too!" said the ant.
But, they did not like the bad dog.

One day, the cat and the ant sat on a rock.
The sun was hot. It was a nice day.
Then, the cat saw the bad dog.

"Oh, no!" said the cat. "The bad dog will eat me!"
"I will not let the bad dog hurt you," said the ant.

The cat ran. The bad dog ran after her.
The ant ran after the bad dog. They ran and ran.
"Help!" cried the cat.

"I will help you!" said the ant. The ant ran fast.
He jumped on the bad dog. He bit the bad dog HARD.

"OW!" yelled the bad dog. "An ant bit me!"
"I will bite you again," said the ant. "Go away!"
The bad dog ran away.

"Thank you!" said the cat. "You are a good friend."
"I am a good ant," said the ant.
"And, that was a BAD dog!"

Name _____

Cat and Dog: Activity Page

Directions: Color the picture that matches the sentence.

This is a cat.	The dog ran away.

The ant and the cat are friends.	The dog ran after the cat.

Poem Title:

The Mole

⊖G •⊖G •⊖G •⊖G •⊖G •⊖G •⊖G •⊖G •⊖G •⊖G •⊖G •⊖G •⊖G •⊖G •⊖G •⊖G •⊖G •⊖G •⊖G •⊖G •⊖G •⊖G •⊖G •

Sight Words Included:

all

am

can

down

on

over

under

up

Looking at Sight Words

1. Make copies of the poem (pages 21–22). Ask students to find and circle the following sight words that are featured in this poem: *all, am, can, down, on, over, under, up*.

2. Write the featured sight words on lined writing paper, leaving space after each word. Make a copy of the featured words for each student. Have students trace the words and then write them.

3. Look for other sight words in the poem: *a, big, eat, I, the, to*. You can also work with students on these words, or set the poem aside to use again when some of these words are introduced in later stories and poems. See the Table of Contents on pages 3 and 4 to find in which story or poem each word is featured.

Playing with Sight Words

1. Make copies of pages 23 and 24. Have students work in pairs or individually to complete the activities.

2. Copy page 25 for each student. Have students complete the page and color the pictures.

3. Ask students, "Which words start the same way?" Speak pairs of words as a warm-up, inviting students to indicate if the words start with the same sound: *am/and*; *up/under*; *down/brown*; *over/hole*; *on/onto*; *can/man*. Next, tell students to think of additional words that start the same way as each of the featured sight words. Write the words on the board as students brainstorm. To make this into a game, divide the class into teams. Students may take turns calling out words as you list them on the board.

Follow-Up Activities

1. Make a bulletin board display of animals that live underground. Find pictures of groundhogs, worms, chipmunks, prairie dogs, tarantulas, and other animals (including moles). Post signs with easy-to-read facts about each animal. Use lots of sight words!

2. Share a book about moles, such as a book from the Mole Sisters series by Roslyn Schwartz, with your class.

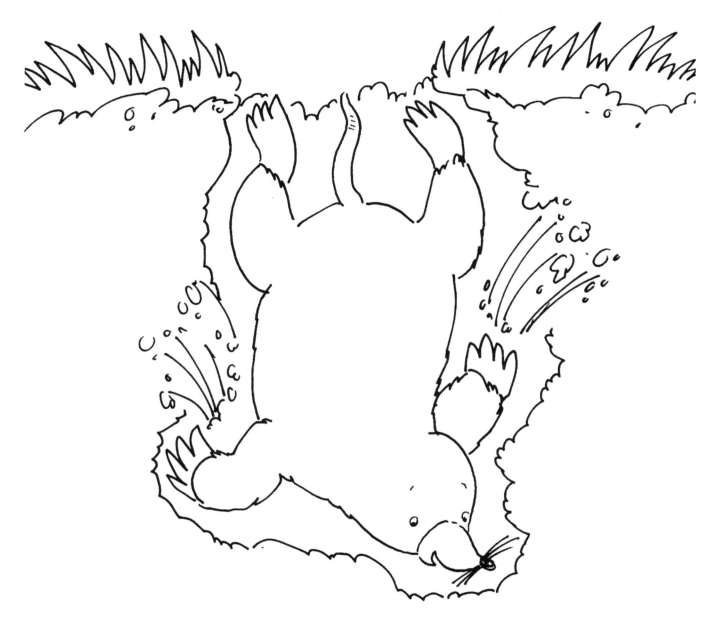

The Mole

I am a mole.
I can dig a big hole.
I dig under a bone.
I dig over a stone.
I dig up! I dig down!
I dig all around.

It is fun, I have found,
To live under the ground.
Come on down! Come see me.
I live under a tree.
I will cook you a bee.
We can eat worms and tea!

Tic-Tac-Toe

Circle the letters that spell "**can**."

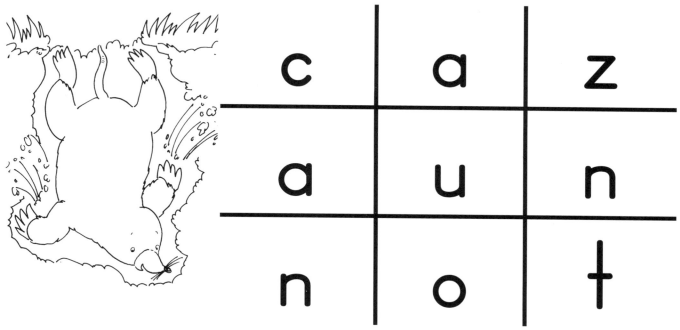

c	a	z
a	u	n
n	o	t

Word Search

Circle the words "**am**."

g	a	m	t
z	m	s	a
a	m	w	m
m	e	n	d

Name _____

Missing Letters

Fill in the missing letters to write "**all**."

Coloring Words

Color all of the pictures that have the word "**on**."

The Mole: Activity Page

Directions: Help Mole! Circle the word that shows where Mole is digging in each picture.

under   over

up   down

up   down

under   over

under   over

up   down

Story Title:

Monster Time

⊕G •⊕G •⊕G •⊕G •⊕G •⊕G •⊕G •⊕G •⊕G •⊕G •⊕G •⊕G •⊕G •⊕G •⊕G •⊕G •⊕G •⊕G •⊕G •⊕G •⊕G •⊕G •

Sight Words Included:

ate

blue

brown

came

eat

good

green

house

in

orange

out

please

red

said

thank

yellow

Looking at Sight Words

1. Make copies of the story (pages 27–32). Cut each page apart along the dashed line, assemble the story's pages in order, and staple it along the left edge. Ask students to find and circle the following sight words that are featured in this story: *ate, blue, brown, came, eat, good, green, house, in, orange, out, please, red, said, thank, yellow.*

2. Ask students to group the featured sight words into sets. Work as a class or in small groups to find the adjectives (e.g., color words), verbs, and directional words. *Please* and *thank* can go into their own category. *House* will be the only noun unless you would like to include other sight words found in the story such as *ball, time,* and *tree.*

3. Look for other sight words in the story: *big, do, like, no, not, the, time, to, tree, with, yes.* You can also work with students on these words, or set the story aside to use again when some of these words are introduced in later stories and poems. See the Table of Contents on pages 3 and 4 to find in which story or poem each word is featured.

Playing with Sight Words

1. Make copies of pages 33 and 34. Have students work in pairs or individually to complete the activities.

2. Use the flannel board patterns on pages 35–37 to help students retell the story of the monster's visit. Be sure they use the color words and other featured sight words as they tell the story.

Follow-Up Activities

1. Make a monster menu! Pretend that your class is opening a monster restaurant. What would the monsters like to eat? Include plenty of color words to describe menu items. Make copies of your finished menu. Let students illustrate their menus with pictures of the menu selections—and monsters, of course!

2. Write a group story about another monster visit. Talk about what might happen if the monster was sleepy or thirsty. What if he wanted to go to the park or to school?

Monster Time

CRUNCH!

The monster came to our house. I let him in.
"Would you like something to eat?" I asked.
"Yes, please." said the monster.
Then, he ate our orange chair!

- -

nibble munch

"Please do not eat the chairs," I said.
"OK," he said. Then, he ate Mom's yellow coat!

"Please do not eat our coats," I said.
"OK," he said. Next, he ate our brown table!

"I think you have had lots to eat," I said.
"We can go out and play now."
"OK," said the monster.

We went out. "You can ride my bike," I said.
"It is the red one."

- -

"Thank you," said the monster. He sat on the bike.
WHOOSH! My red bike was flat!
"Sorry," he said.

"We can play on the swings," I said.
The monster sat on a swing. BANG!
The swing fell down. "Sorry," he said.

page 8

"We can play with that big blue ball," I said.
"OK," he said. He threw the ball. CRASH!
The ball broke our window.
"Sorry," said the monster.

"Can I please have more to eat?"
He looked at our big green tree. "That looks good."
"Sorry," I said.

"I think it is time for you to go home now."
"OK," said the monster.

"Did you have a coat?" I asked.
"No," he said. "I ate it before I got here."

page 12

We walked to the gate.
"Thank you for the nice time," said the monster.
"That chair was very good!"

Name _____

Word Search

Circle the words "**eat**"
and "**ate**."

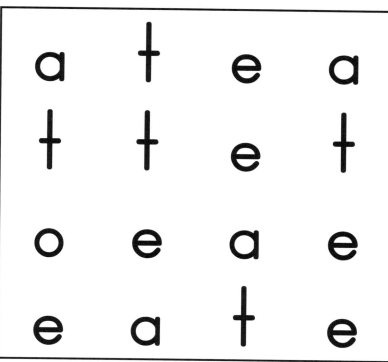

a   t   e   a

t   t   e   t

o   e   a   e

e   a   t   e

Pyramid Words

Build a pyramid for the word "**thank**."

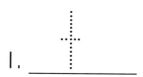

1. ___ t ___

2. _____ _____

3. _____ _____ _____

4. _____ _____ _____ _____

5. _____ _____ _____ _____ _____

Name _____

Color Words

Color each picture to match the color word.

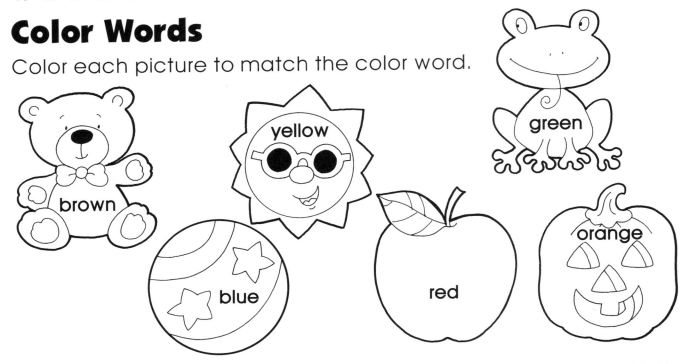

Choose the Right Word

Circle the word to match each picture.

Monster Time: Flannel Board Patterns

Directions: Use these patterns to make flannel-board storytelling pieces for the story on pages 27–32. Copy the patterns onto card stock and color specific pieces as follows: orange chair, yellow raincoat, brown table, red bike, blue ball, and green tree. Then, cut the pieces out and laminate them for durability. Finally, glue sandpaper or place self-stick hook-and-loop tape on the back of each piece.

Monster Time: Flannel Board Patterns, continued

Monster Time: Flannel Board Patterns, continued

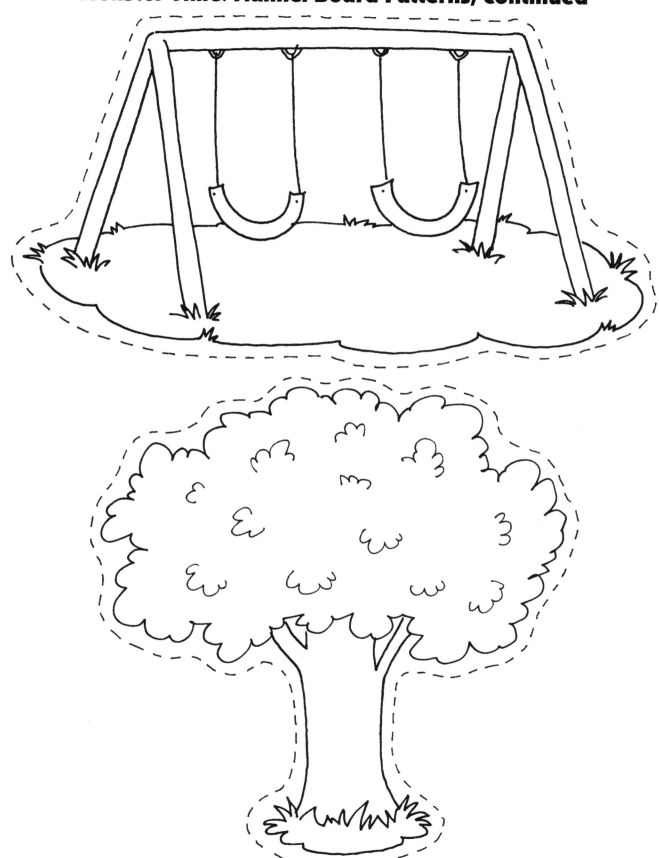

Poem Title:

Little Sister

⊕G •⊕G •⊕G •⊕G •⊕G •⊕G •⊕G •⊕G •⊕G •⊕G •⊕G •⊕G •⊕G •⊕G •⊕G •⊕G •⊕G •⊕G •⊕G •⊕G •⊕G •⊕G •

Sight Words Included:

ask

for

give

that

this

want

when

Looking at Sight Words

1. Make copies of the poem (page 39). Ask students to find and circle the following sight words that are featured in this poem: *ask, for, give, that, this, want, when.*

2. Ask students to count how many lines start with the same word in the poem. (Eight lines start with *I* and two lines start with *give.*)

3. Look for other sight words in the poem: *I, me, say, you.* You can also work with students on these words, or set the poem aside to use again when some of these words are introduced in later stories and poems. See the Table of Contents on pages 3 and 4 to find in which story or poem each word is featured.

Playing with Sight Words

1. Make copies of pages 40 and 41. Have students work in pairs or individually to complete the activities.

2. Copy page 42 for each student. Have students complete the page and color the pictures.

3. Play a "Let's Change This Word!" game. Ask students what word they could make if they changed the first letter or sound in *that.* What if they changed the first letter of *give*? What words could students make by adding a first letter to *ask*? Be sure to write each sight word on the board as you play so that students see and read the original word and gain familiarity with it.

Follow-Up Activities

1. Discuss what three sight words make asking for things more polite than the way the little sister does in the poem? (*Please* and *thank you*!) Have students role-play shopping in a store and asking for something using these words.

2. Ask students if they have younger brothers or sisters. What do they like about their siblings? What things would they like to change?

Little Sister

I ask for this!

I ask for that!

When I go to the store,

I say, "Give me that!

I want this doll,

I want that hat!

I want this ball,

I want that bat!

Can you hear me?

I want that!

Give me, give me,

Give me THAT!"

Name _____

Color the Words

Color the engines that have the word "**ask**."

Pyramid Words

Build a pyramid for the word "**give**."

1. __g__

2. _____ _____

3. _____ _____ _____

4. _____ _____ _____ _____

Letter Maze   Circle the letters that spell "**want**."

Word Search

Circle the words "**when**."

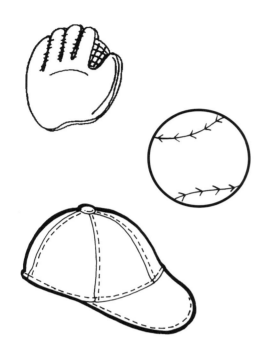

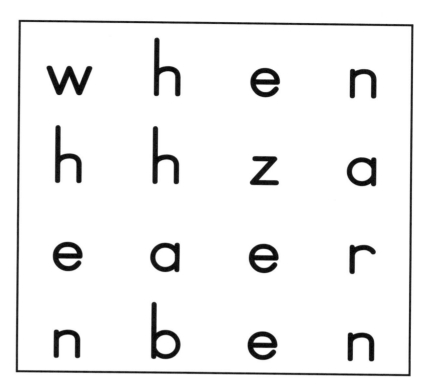

Finish the Sentence

Write the word "**for**" to finish each sentence.

1. I will ask _____ a new toy.

2. I had a hot dog _____ lunch.

3. I use a pen _____ writing.

Name_____

Little Sister: Activity Page

Directions: Time to go to the toy store! Circle the word "**this**" or "**that**" to choose one toy in each box. Then, color the toys you chose.

this	or	that
this	or	that
this	or	that
this	or	that
this	or	that
this	or	that

Sam and Jen

Sight Words Included:

by

come

do

get

go

here

jump

no

ride

run

so

then

there

to

tree

yes

Looking at Sight Words

1. Make copies of the story (pages 44–46). Cut each page apart along the dashed line, assemble the story's pages in order, and staple it along the left edge. Ask students to find and circle the following sight words that are featured in this story: *by, come, do, get, go, here, jump, no, ride, run, so, then, there, to, tree, yes.*

2. Make copies of page 47 for each student. Help students cut out and color the Jen stick-puppet shapes and then attach them to sticks. Read the story out loud while students hold up the correct stick puppets to show whether Jen is saying "Yes, Sam!" and "Good dog!" or "No, Sam!" and "Bad dog!" based on her expressions. You can also write the selected sight words on the board and point to them as you read.

3. Look for other sight words in the story: *a, am, be, dog, good, I, out, say(s), the, want.* You can also work with students on these words, or set the story aside to use again when some of these words are introduced in later stories or poems. See the Table of Contents on pages 3 and 4 to find in which story or poem each word is featured.

Playing with Sight Words

1. Make copies of pages 48 and 49. Have students work in pairs or individually to complete the activities.

2. Make copies of the maze on page 50. Have students circle the selected sight words to find the correct path "home." They can also color the pictures.

3. Play a game based on the story. Instead of "Simon says," play "Jen says." To reinforce students' sight word recognition after each statement, hold up a sign labeled either "yes" or "no" to show if the students should have made the action or not.

Follow-Up Activities

1. Take a field trip to a dog obedience school or ask a dog trainer or Humane Society representative to make a class visit to show students how to train pets. Before completing the activity, be sure to ask families' permission and inquire about students' animal allergies.

2. Take a poll in your class. Who likes cats? Who likes dogs? Tally the number of votes for each type of pet.

Sam and Jen

I am a dog. I try to be good. But, it is so hard!
I run with Jen. She says, "Yes, Sam! Good dog!"
But then, I run after a cat.
Jen says, "No, Sam! Bad dog!"

I lie down next to the chair.
Jen says, "Yes, Sam. Good dog!"
But then, I run out the door.
I want to lie down by the tree.
Jen says, "No, Sam! Bad dog! Come here!"

page 2

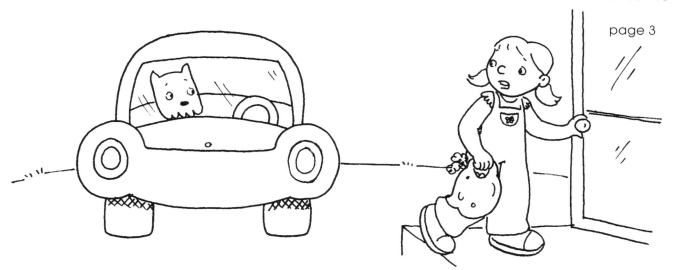

I ride in the car with Jen. We go to the store.
She says, "Stay there, Sam. Good dog!"
But then, we go home.
I do not want to get out of the car.
Jen says, "Bad dog, Sam! Come here."

- -

Jen calls me.

She says, "Come, Sam!" I go to her.
She says, "Yes, Sam! Good dog!"
Then, I am happy to see her. I jump up.
Jen says, "No, Sam! Bad dog! Get down."

Yes, Sam. No, Sam. Come here.
Stay there. Good dog! Bad dog!
I hear these things all day long.
Do you see why it is all so hard?
Am I a good dog or a bad dog?

I am not sure.
But, I am sure of one thing.
I know Jen loves me.
She takes me for runs.
We go on walks.
We ride in her car.
She feeds me good food.
She hugs me.
I have lots of toys.
I have a nice bed.
It is a good thing I have Jen!
She knows more than I do.

She knows what makes a good dog or a bad dog.
So, she knows what I should do!

Sam and Jen: Stick-Puppet Patterns

Directions: Use the stick-puppet patterns below to help tell the story "Sam and Jen" on pages 44–46. Copy, color, and cut out each pattern. Attach each figure to a craft stick with glue or double-sided tape.

Name _____

Letter Maze   Circle the letters that spell "**tree**."

Pyramid Words

Build a pyramid for the word "**come**."

1. ______

2. _____ _____

3. _____ _____ _____

4. _____ _____ _____ _____

Name _____

Coloring Words

Color all of the dogs that have the word "**there**."

Finish the Sentence

Write the word "**yes**" or "**no**" to finish each sentence.

1. I said, "_____!
    I like dogs!"

2. _____, we do
    not have a dog.

3. _____ one
    saw Sam today.

Sam and Jen: Activity Page

Directions: Help Sam find Jen. Follow these words to find the right path:

by	come	do	get	go	here	jump	no
ride	run	so	then	there	to	tree	yes

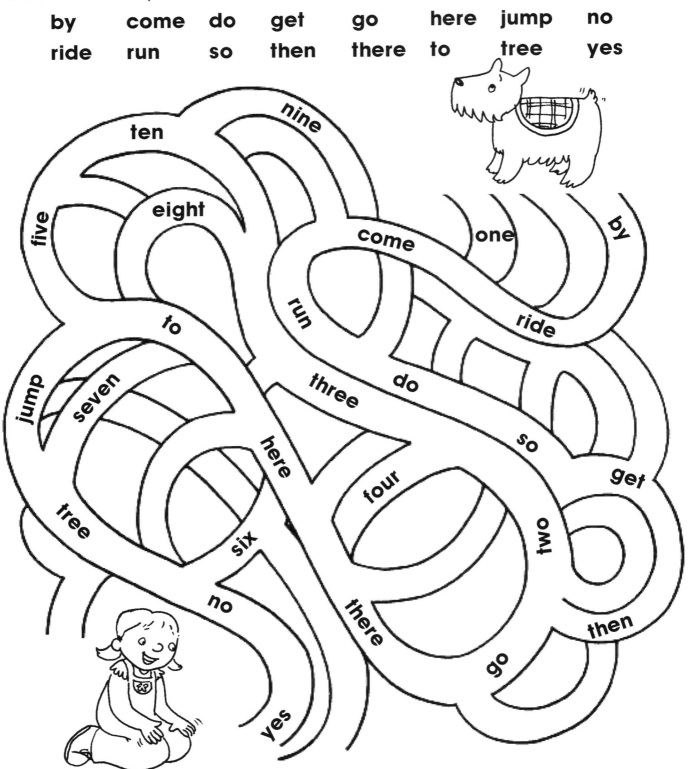

Poem Title:

A Friend for Bear

OG •OG •OG •OG •OG •OG •OG •OG •OG •OG •OG •OG •OG •OG •OG •OG •OG •OG •OG •OG •OG •OG •OG •

Sight Words Included:

be

could

five

from

is

who

will

would

Looking at Sight Words

1. Make copies of the poem (pages 52–53). Ask students to find and circle the following sight words that are featured in this poem: *be, could, five, from, is, who, will, would.*

2. Model writing the individual letters of each sight word on the board. Point out the difference between the words *be* and *bee.* Then, ask students to practice writing the words.

3. Look for other sight words in the poem: *good, have, I, in, my, the, there, to, under.* You can also work with students on these words, or set the poem aside to use again when some of these words are introduced in later stories and poems. See the Table of Contents on pages 3 and 4 to find in which story or poem each word is featured.

Playing with Sight Words

1. Make large-sized templates of the featured sight words and copy them. Have students do rainbow writing, tracing the letters of the words with their favorite colors.

2. Copy pages 54 and 55 for each student. Have students complete the pages and color the pictures.

3. Use the flannel board patterns on pages 56 and 57 to help students retell the story of Bear's search for bee friends.

Follow-Up Activities

1. Have a honey-tasting happening! Bring honey to class and let students sample it on bread or crackers. Before completing this food activity, be sure to ask families' permission and inquire about students' food allergies. See if you can also find a honeycomb to show the class.

2. Learn more about bees. Display pictures of hives. Talk about the facts that bees live in a "society" with workers and a queen and that bees hibernate.

A Friend for Bear

Is there a bee
Who will be my friend?
I live in the cave
Around the bend.
I sit in the sun
Under the trees.
I could be
A good friend to bees.

I love sweet honey
From the hive.
That's why I want bee friends—
Maybe five!
I have room in my cave
For the bees to stay.
If they would bring honey,
They could stay all day!

Tic-Tac-Toe

Circle the letters that spell "**who**."

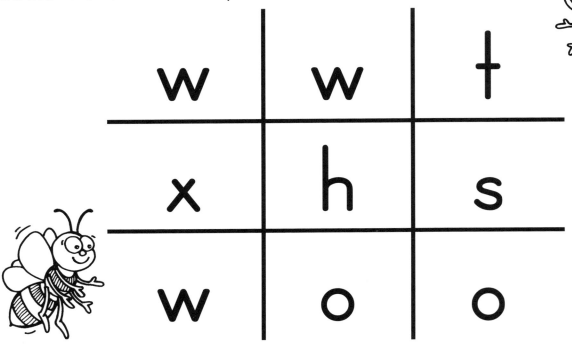

w	w	t
x	h	s
w	o	o

Letter Maze

Circle the letters that spell "**five**."

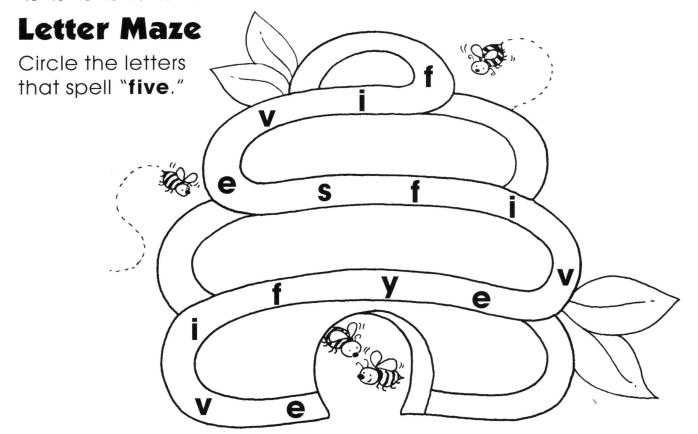

Missing Letters

Fill in the missing letters to write "**will**," "**who**," and "**from**."

w ___ ___ l

f ___ ___ o ___

___ ___ ___ o

Finish the Sentence

Write the word "**could**" or "**would**" to finish each sentence.

1. I said, "_____ we
    please see the bees?"

2. Who _____ like
    some honey?

3. We _____ eat
    the honey now!

A Friend for Bear: Flannel Board Patterns

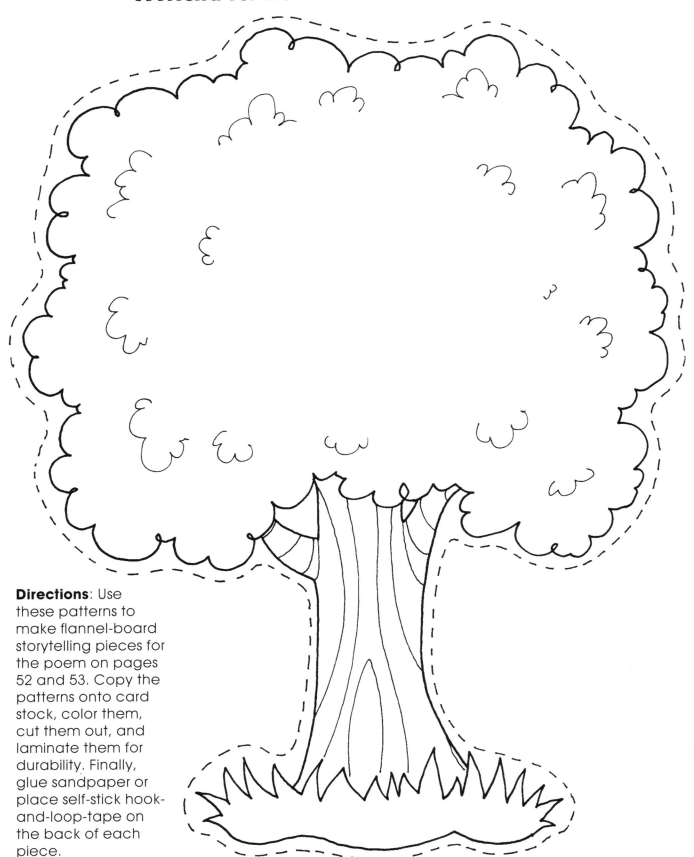

Directions: Use these patterns to make flannel-board storytelling pieces for the poem on pages 52 and 53. Copy the patterns onto card stock, color them, cut them out, and laminate them for durability. Finally, glue sandpaper or place self-stick hook-and-loop-tape on the back of each piece.

A Friend for Bear: Flannel Board Patterns, continued

Story Title:

Too Many Pets?

🐶G •🐶G •🐶G •🐶G •🐶G •🐶G •🐶G •🐶G •🐶G •🐶G •🐶G •🐶G •🐶G •🐶G •🐶G •🐶G •🐶G •🐶G •🐶G •🐶G •🐶G •🐶G •

Sight Words Included:

but

dad

did

eight

every

four

how

just

mom

nine

of

one

seven

six

ten

them

three

too

two

was

Looking at Sight Words

1. Make copies of the story (pages 59–63). Cut each page apart along the dashed line, assemble the story's pages in order, and staple it along the left edge. Ask students to find and circle the following sight words that are featured in this story: *but, dad, did, eight, every, four, how, just, mom, nine, of, one, seven, six, ten, them, three, too, two, was*.

2. Ask students to look for rhyming words in the story. Find groups of them (*two, too, do; Sal, Gal, Pal; no, go, so*) and list them on the board. Have students use the words to write a poem as a class.

3. Look for other sight words in the story: *are, big, five, have, I, is, it, let, little, many, said, will*. You can also work with students on these words, or set the story aside to use again when some of these words are introduced in later stories and poems. See the Table of Contents on pages 3 and 4 to find in which story or poem each word is featured.

Playing with Sight Words

1. Make copies of pages 64 and 65. Have students work in pairs or individually to complete the activities.

2. Make copies of page 66. Ask students to complete the page and color the picture.

3. Play a matching game with the number words found in the story. Make large cards with a number word on each one. Have students match the number word cards to corresponding groups of objects and to numerals written on the board. You can play this game in teams if you like.

Follow-Up Activities

1. Make "dream pet" lists. Ask what pets students would most like to own. Dinosaurs? One hundred dalmatians? Have students illustrate their lists for a bulletin board display.

2. In a storytelling circle, have students tell stories about pets. The stories can be about their own pets, a neighbor's or friend's pet, or a pet they read about in a book.

page 2

I love pets!
Mom and Dad say I have too many pets.
I do have a lot of pets. Here is how it started.

My first pet was Sal. She is a big dog.
Then, Sal had two puppies! I called them Gal and Pal.
"But, now you have three dogs!" said Mom.
"Please let me keep them," I said.
"I will feed them every day. I will take them on walks."

- -

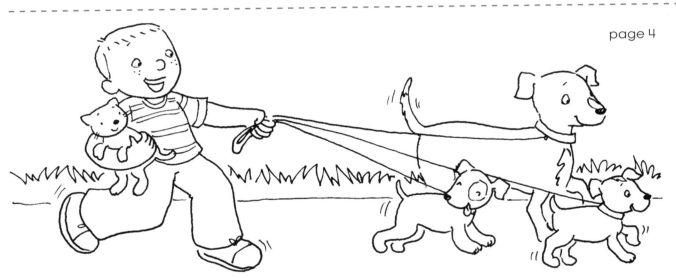

One day, I took Sal, Pal, and Gal on a walk.
They ran. They chased a little cat.
The cat did not have a home. I had to help her.
So, I took her with me. I called her Kay.
That made four pets.

I only had four pets for a little while.
Then one night, Kay had five kittens.
"Six cats!" said Dad. "That is too many!"
"Now, you have nine pets!" said Mom.

"They are all good pets," I said.
"Sal, Pal, and Gal like Kay. They like her kittens.
They play with each other. Please let me keep them."

It was the start of summer.
My teacher asked me, "Can you take care of our class pets?
Just for the summer?"
"Yes!" I said. I did not think.

Mom came to pick me up. I had two mice.
I had four little frogs. And, I had one big snake.
"Thomas! You have seven more pets!" said Mom.
She looked sick.

"It is just for the summer," I said.
"But . . ." Mom could not even talk.
She just looked at the cages. Now, I have nine pets.
And, I have seven guest pets! I have to work hard.

Kay must not go in the room with the mice.
Gal and Pal bark at the frogs.
The kittens are scared of the snake.
Mom and Dad shake their heads.
Dad says, "No more pets until you are eight!"
"No more pets until you are TEN!" says Mom.
But, I am so happy! This is the best summer ever.

Name _____

Blend the Word

Draw a line to make the word "**them**."

Word Search

Circle the letters that spell "**just**."

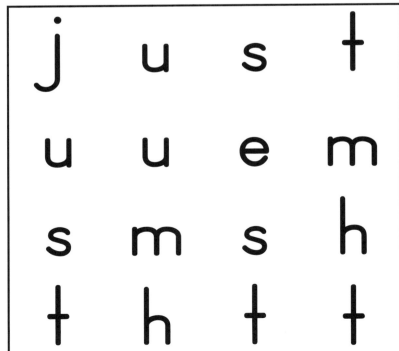

Missing Letters

Fill in the missing letters to write "**how**," "**was**," "**did**," and "**but**."

Coloring Words

Color the pictures that have the word "**mom**" or "**dad**."

Name _____

Too Many Pets? Counting Fun Page

Directions: Count each group of pets. Write the word that shows how many of each pet. Then, color the picture!

Use these words: **one   two   three   four   five   six   seven   eight   nine**

Poem Title:

Cool Shoes

ⓔⓖ •

Sight Words Included:

are

black

has

have

he

his

or

purple

she

white

with

Looking at Sight Words

1. Make copies of the poem (pages 68–69). Ask students to find and circle the following sight words that are featured in this poem: *are, black, has, have, he, his, or, purple, she, white, with.*

2. Tell students you are going to stretch words out, and you want them to "snap the words back." Say each featured sight word in the poem slowly (*h-h-h-h . . . a-a-a-a . . . v-v-v-v; h-h-h-h . . . e-e-e-e;* etc.). Ask students to blend the sounds back together so that they can tell you what word you have stretched.

3. Look for other sight words in the poem: *and, brown, can, for, go, in, of, orange, out, red, so, them, you.* You can also work with students on these words, or set the poem aside to use again when some of these words are introduced in later stories and poems. See the Table of Contents on pages 3 and 4 to find in which story or poem each word is featured.

Playing with Sight Words

1. Have a color word relay race. On index cards, print the color words featured in this poem—*black, purple,* and *white*—as well as color words that students have already learned—*blue, brown, green, orange, red,* and *yellow.* Organize students into three or four teams. Hand each team one card at a time and have them work together to find a classroom object of that color and place the card on it. The first team that places all of their cards correctly wins.

2. Copy pages 70 and 71 for each student. Have students complete the page and color the pictures.

3. Make copies of page 72. Ask students to complete the activity. Be sure to have them refer back to the poem to match the right colors to the shoes and names.

Follow-Up Activities

1. Ask each student to draw a picture of a favorite pair of shoes.

2. Set up a shoe store! Use doll shoes or shoes that students bring into class. Price each pair of shoes and have students shop and then add up their totals.

Cool Shoes

I have some cool shoes,
And you have some, too.
Jamal has some cool shoes
And so does May Lou.
Shoes can be fancy, or
Shoes can be plain.
Shoes can go out in
The sun or the rain.
Jen's shoes are purple,
And Pat's shoes are black.

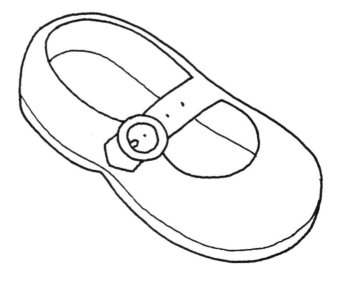

Juan lost his white shoes,
But he got them back.
Teresa has pink shoes
She uses for dancing.
I dream of orange shoes—
I want them for prancing!
Chen has brown shoes
That he likes a lot.
Kai loves her red shoes
With big bows and dots!

Name_____

Word Search

Circle the words "**have**."

Blend the Word

Draw a line to make the word "**black**."

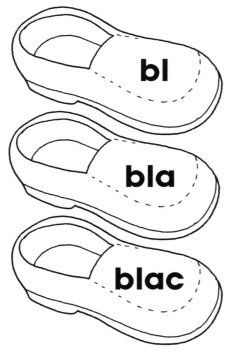

bl

bla

blac

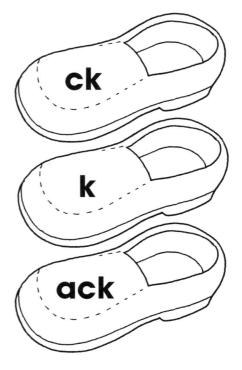

ck

k

ack

Scrambled Words

Unscramble the letters to spell the word "**white**."

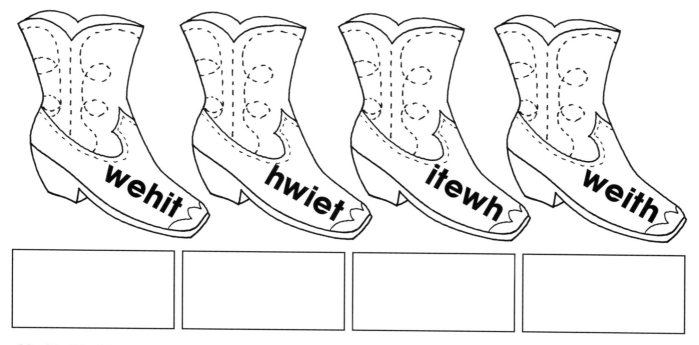

Coloring Words

Color the shoes with the words "**he**," "**she**," and "**his**."

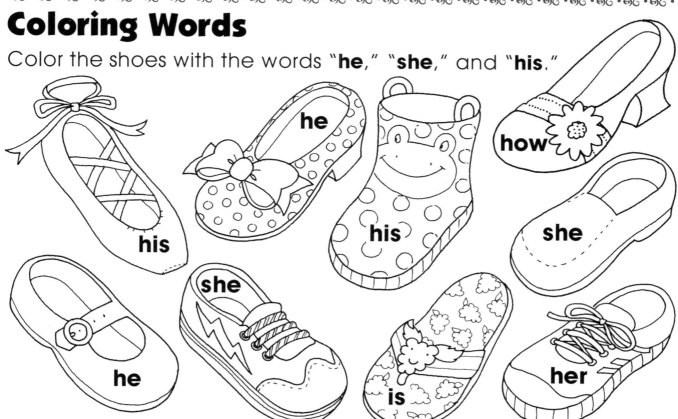

Cool Shoes: Coloring Fun Page

Directions: Color each pair of shoes. Use the poem to help you.
Write the color word of the shoes on the line.

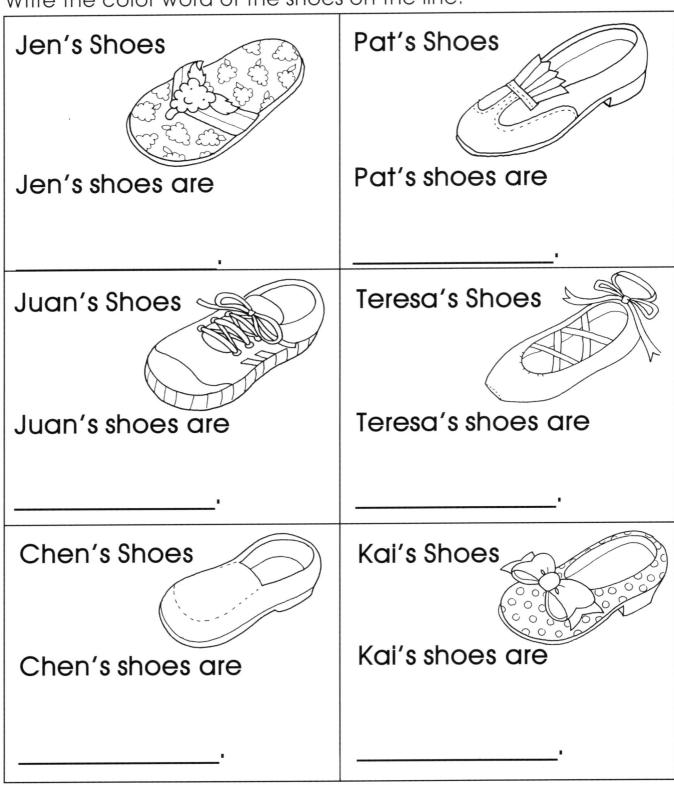

Jen's Shoes

Jen's shoes are

_____.

Pat's Shoes

Pat's shoes are

_____.

Juan's Shoes

Juan's shoes are

_____.

Teresa's Shoes

Teresa's shoes are

_____.

Chen's Shoes

Chen's shoes are

_____.

Kai's Shoes

Kai's shoes are

_____.

About the Zoo

Sight Words
Included:

about

at

big

each

find

it

its

little

long

look

make

people

soon

take

their

they

time

walk

Looking at Sight Words

1. Make copies of the story (pages 74–76). Cut each page apart along the dashed line, assemble the story's pages in order, and staple it along the left edge. Ask students to find and circle the following sight words that are featured in this story: *about, at, big, each, find, it, its, little, long, look, make, people, soon, take, their, they, time, walk.*

2. Make alphabet letter cards to spell each of the featured sight words. Create a set for each group of students. Have students work in teams to assemble the shorter featured sight words with the cards. Work on the longer words (*about, people, little,* etc.) together as a class.

3. Look for other sight words in the story: *can, could, day, do, in, now, the, then, to, who, you.* You can also work with students on these words, or set the story aside to use again when some of these words are introduced in later stories and poems. See the Table of Contents on pages 3 and 4 to find in which story or poem each word is featured.

Playing with Sight Words

1. Copy pages 77 and 78 for each student. Have students complete the pages and color the pictures.

2. Make copies of pages 79–81 for each student. Help students cut out and color the stick-puppet shapes and then attach them to sticks. Read the poem out loud or do a choral reading. Students can use their stick puppets to act out the poem.

3. Play a word families game. Ask students to stand up when they hear a word that rhymes with the featured sight word. Name a sight word and then give them two or three choices for the word. Examples: *at, can, cat; long, log, strong; take, cane, cake; big, pig, pick; look, like, book;* etc.

Follow-Up Activities

1. Design a zoo. Make a map with outlines of empty pens and habitat areas. Then, let each student lay out his or her own zoo and draw the animals for each exhibit.

2. Take a virtual field trip! Many zoos have great online sites, even including live Web cams of animal exhibits. Let students explore a zoo on the Web. Talk about what they have learned.

About the Zoo

Do you know who lives at the zoo? I do!
I could spend all day at the zoo.

You will find the monkeys on their little island.
They like to make long leaps in their trees.

Take a long look at the lions. They are like big cats.
They move about in their den. They nap.
They yawn. Then, they roar!

Each big bear has its own cave.
They all walk about in the sun.
The people wave to the bears.

There is a big cage for the birds.
Many kinds of birds are there. They fly and dive.
They sing. Some of the birds are green.
Some are red. Some are blue.

page 6

Take time to walk to the little farm.
You can hold a rabbit. You can pat a pig.
You can pet a goat. It is a lot of fun.
Now, you know about the zoo, too!
We can make a plan to go there soon.

Tic-Tac-Toe

Circle the letters that spell "**big**."

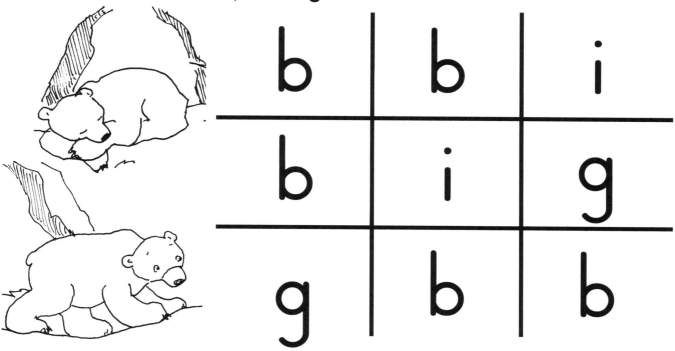

b	b	i
b	i	g
g	b	b

Blend the Word

Draw a line to make the word "**their**."

the

th

t

heir

eir

ir

Name _____

Scrambled Words

Unscramble the letters to spell the word "**people**."

opepel

plepeo

pleeop

elpoep

Writing Words

Write "**big**" or "**little**" under each animal to show its size.

Directions: Use the stick-puppet patterns to help tell the story "About the Zoo" on pages 74–76. Copy, color, and cut out each pattern. Attach each figure to a craft stick with glue or double-sided tape.

About the Zoo: Stick-Puppet Patterns, continued

Poem Title:

Play Day

Sight Words Included:

and

boy

call

day

him

if

must

not

play

say

Looking at Sight Words

1. Make copies of the poem (pages 83–86). Ask students to find and circle the following sight words that are featured in this poem: *and, boy, call, day, him, if, must, not, play, say.*

2. Tell students you want to change the first sound of a featured word. For example, write the word *not* on the board. Then say, "Listen to the word *not*. Change the /n/ sound to /d/. What word have we made?"

3. Look for other sight words in the poem: *ball, big, give, go, good, has, have, he, I, is, little, take, to.* You can also work with students on these words, or set the poem aside to use again when some of these words are introduced in later stories and poems. See the Table of Contents on pages 3 and 4 to find in which story or poem each word is featured.

Playing with Sight Words

1. Working as a class, write a poem or song together using the featured sight words. To help spur ideas, have students tell stories about a boy who liked to play all day, a boy who was told he must not play, etc. Then, choose a story idea to turn into a rhyme.

2. Copy pages 87 and 88 for each student. Have students complete the page and color the pictures.

3. Make copies of page 89. Ask students to complete the activity. Then, create more words and phrases featuring sight words from this poem and ask students to act them out.

Follow-Up Activities

1. Share a funny book with the class about a difficult situation with a younger child, such as *My Brother, the Brat* by Kirsten Hall or a selection from the classic *Ramona the Pest* by Beverly Cleary.

2. Talk with students about playing with younger children. Discuss why it is important to be patient and share.

Play Day

I must not bother Peter
When he comes to play.
I have to give him my toys.
He has to have his way.

He is my little cousin,
And I'm the boy who's big.
I have to give him my treats,
And see him be a pig!

If I say, "Do not do that!"
He will cry and call.
He gets to use my new bat.
He gets to take my ball.

I have to be nice all day,
And never tell him "no."
And when Play Day is over,
It's good to see him go!

Pyramid Words

Build a pyramid for the word "**must**."

1.  m
2. _____
3. _____
4. _____

Tic-Tac-Toe

Circle the words "**not**."

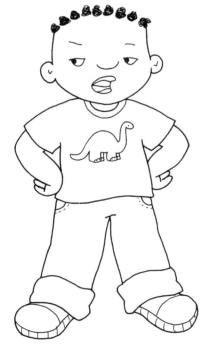

not	no	nod
nor	not	no
now	nor	not

Name _____

Coloring Words

Color the balls that have the words "**day**," "**say**," and "**play**."

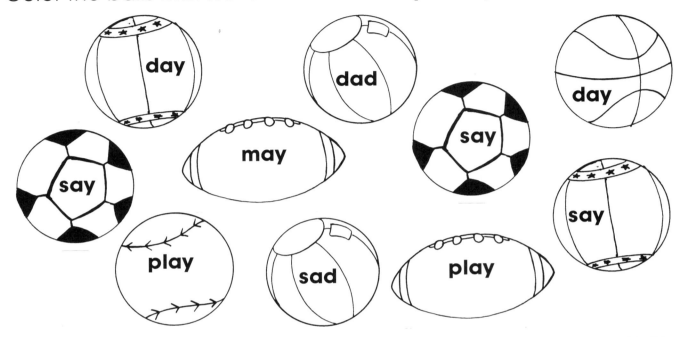

Missing Letters

Fill in the missing letters to write "**and**," "**call**," and "**him**."

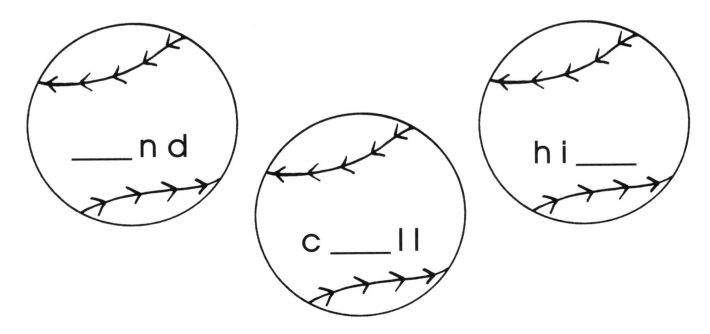

Play Day: Sight Word Meanings

Directions: Circle the correct picture to match each word or words.

play

the boy

day

call

must not

say hi

Story Title:

Ball Game

⊙G •⊙G •⊙G •⊙G •⊙G •⊙G •⊙G •⊙G •⊙G •⊙G •⊙G •⊙G •⊙G •⊙G •⊙G •⊙G •⊙G •⊙G •⊙G •⊙G •⊙G •⊙G •

Sight Words Included:

again

any

ball

first

fly

had

many

may

some

went

were

Looking at Sight Words

1. Make copies of the story (pages 91–93). Cut each page apart along the dashed line, assemble the story's pages in order, and staple it along the left edge. Ask students to find and circle the following sight words that are featured in this story: *again, any, ball, first, fly, had, many, may, some, went, were.*

2. Together as a class, invent a story about another subject (such as a play date in a park) using the same sight words featured in this story.

3. Look for other sight words in the story: *been, call(ed), is, it, me, now, people, said, then, there, we, yes.* You can also work with students on these words, or set the story aside to use again when some of these words are introduced in later stories and poems. See the Table of Contents on pages 3 and 4 to find in which story or poem each word is featured.

Playing with Sight Words

1. Copy pages 94 and 95. Have students complete the pages and color the pictures.

2. Make copies of page 96 for each student. Have students finish the picture by adding details and then color their completed pictures. Review the specifics of the story (the people sitting near Beth and Dad, the types of food the vendors are selling, the moment Beth catches the ball, etc.) before students add them to the drawing.

3. Play Sight Word Baseball! Clear out a large area of the room and put down a home plate plus first, second, and third bases made of construction paper or cardboard. For each student "batter," write one of the featured sight words on the board or use a flash card. If the word is read correctly, the student advances to first base and the next "batter" gets a turn.

Follow-Up Activities

1. Share a story or song (such as "Take Me Out to the Ball Game") about baseball. Have students been to a baseball game? Ask them to tell about their experiences.

2. Have a baseball snack break with popcorn, peanuts, or other "ballpark" food. Before completing this food activity, ask families' permission and inquire about students' food allergies and religious or other food preferences.

Ball Game

My dad took me to a ball game. It was my first time. We went to the ballpark. Many people were there.

The ball game started.
"We may even catch a fly ball," said Dad.

"Is there any food?" I asked.
"Oh, yes!" said Dad.

First, we got hot dogs.
Then, I ate some popcorn.
Then, we had hot dogs again. Then, I had some nuts.

page 5

The game was good. We called. We cheered.
One batter hit the ball hard.
"It is a fly ball!" said Dad. "Here it comes, Beth!"
I got the ball! Many people said, "Good catch" to me.

- -

page 6

I got to take the ball home. I had so much fun.
Our team won! Now, I have been to a ball game.
I want to go back again and again.

Name _____

Letter Connect

Connect the letters that spell "**ball**."

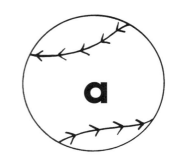
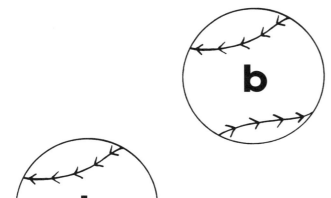

Tic-Tac-Toe

Circle the words "**were**."

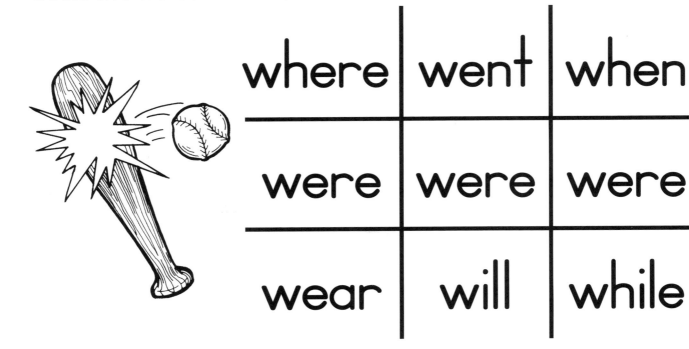

where	went	when
were	were	were
wear	will	while

Scrambled Words

Unscramble the letters to spell the word "**first**."

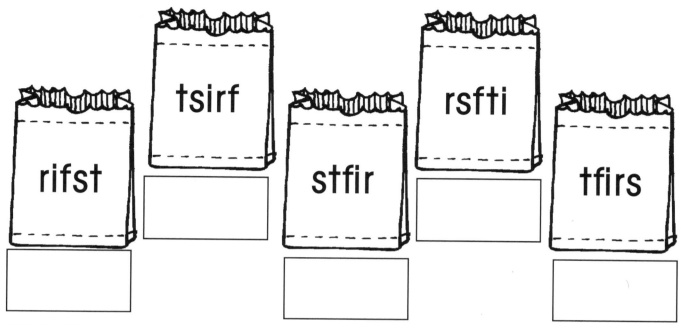

Coloring Words

Color the caps that have the words "**many**," "**may**," and "**any**."

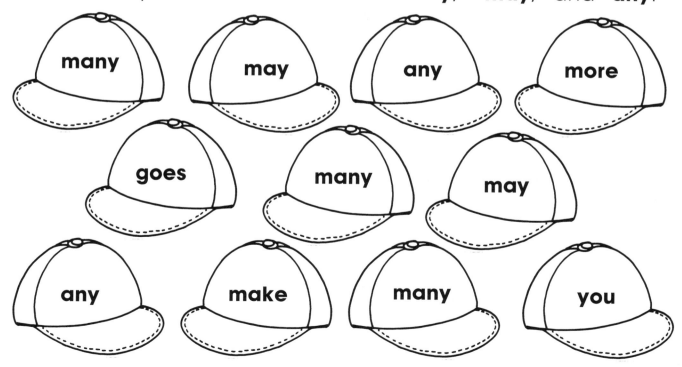

Name _____

Ball Game: Drawing Fun Page

Directions: Dad and Beth are at the ball game. You can go to the game, too! Draw the things that are missing. Then, color the picture.

Poem Title:

Rain Walk

Sight Words Included:

funny

made

pretty

put

saw

school

water

Looking at Sight Words

1. Make copies of the poem (pages 98–99). Ask students to find and circle the following sight words that are featured in this poem: *funny, made, pretty, put, saw, school, water.*

2. Model writing the individual letters of each sight word on the board. Then, ask students to practice writing the words.

3. Look for other sight words in the poem that have already been introduced in previous stories and poems: *all, big, I, in, my, of, on, one, their, to, was, went, were.* You can also work with students on these words. See the Table of Contents on pages 3 and 4 to find in which story or poem each word is featured.

Playing with Sight Words

1. Ask students, "Which words in this poem start with the same letters?" Speak pairs of sight words as a warm-up: *pretty/put; water/went; my/made; saw/school.* Have students call out additional words that start with the same letter as each of the featured sight words. Write words on the board as students brainstorm.

2. Copy pages 100 and 101 for each student. Have students complete the pages and color the pictures.

3. Copy the minibook about rain on pages 102 and 103. Read the story together with students. Then, have students color, cut out, and assemble the pages in order. Help students staple their minibooks. Use the books for additional sight word work.

Follow-Up Activities

1. Write sight words on raindrop shapes and create a bulletin board display. Be sure to include the sight words from "Rain Walk" as well as other weather words.

2. Collect stories and poems about rain. Make copies for students. Then, ask them to go through the stories and poems and underline all of the sight words they find.

Rain Walk

I put on my pretty shoes.
I walk to school each day.
Last night, there was a big rain.
It made me want to play.
SPLASH! I jumped in puddles.
I love the water sound.
SPLASH! I went to each one.
SPLASH! I hit the ground!

The puddles were so much fun,
I did not think at all.
But, I looked funny dripping
With water in the hall.
My pretty shoes were gone.
In their place, I saw
Two big slabs of wet mud,
Like a big dog's paws!

Name _____

Pyramid Words

Build a pyramid for the word "**made**."

1. m_____

2. _____ _____

3. _____ _____ _____

4. _____ _____ _____ _____

Word Tic-Tac-Toe

Circle the words "**saw**."

so	saw	sat
sob	saw	sad
sit	saw	say

Name _____

Coloring Words

Color the umbrellas that have the words "**pretty**," "**school**," and "**funny**."

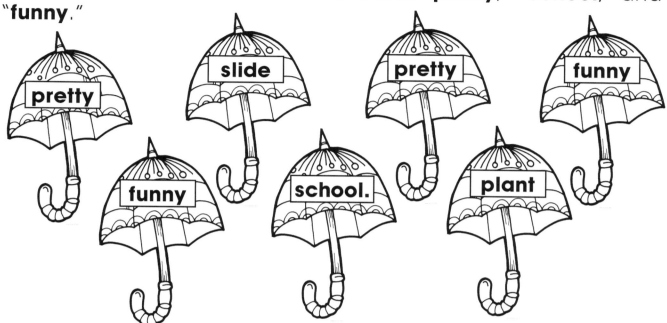

Missing Letters

Fill in the missing letters to write "**water**."

I Like Rain

-2-

The rain is here.

-3-

The rain makes
flowers grow.

They are red
and yellow.

-4-

The rain makes
puddles.

The rain helps
new plants.

The birds drink
rainwater.

The rain is good
for all of us.

I like the rain.

Story Title:

Our New Home

Sight Words Included:

as

help

into

new

now

our

see

these

very

well

Looking at Sight Words

1. Make copies of the story (pages 105–108). Cut each page apart along the dashed line, assemble the story's pages in order, and staple it along the left edge. Ask students to find and circle the following sight words that are featured in this story: *as*, *help*, *into*, *new*, *now*, *our*, *see*, *these*, *very*, *well*.

2. Ask students questions about the story, using sight words in your questions. For example, ask, "Is the home in the story new?" "Is the planet very pretty?" As you say each sight word, write it on the board or hold up a card labeled with each new word you are using.

3. Look for other sight words in the story that have already been introduced in previous stories and poems: *any*, *away*, *by*, *can*, *down*, *eat*, *had*, *it*, *like*, *not*, *saw*, *to*, *too*, *we*, *will*. You can also work with students on these words. See the Table of Contents on pages 3 and 4 to find in which story or poem each word is featured.

Playing with Sight Words

1. Make copies of pages 109 and 110. Have students work in pairs or individually to complete the activities.

2. Use the flannel board patterns on pages 111–114 to help students retell the story of the new home on Planet IK2B3. Be sure they use the featured sight words as they tell the story.

3. Make up another story together about life on Planet IK2B3. What would it be like to fly to school each day? What would happen if the people living on the planet ran out of water dust?

Follow-Up Activities

1. Have students study the planets in our solar system. Discuss which one, besides Earth, would be best on which to live. What would their new homes be like there?

2. Invite students to design a space town! Have them draw pictures of different kinds of buildings and then arrange their ideas in a display.

Our New Home

We moved to a new home.
It is very far away.
It is on Planet 1K2B3.
I saw our new home as we flew to it.
"It is pretty!" I said. "Look at the green sky!"
"I like these red roads," said Mom.

- -

"It is too bad that 1K2B3 does not have any water,"
said Dad. "But, we can eat water dust."
"And, we can drink milk!" I said.

We flew over my new school.

"Look! It has its own jet pad," I said.

"I see they put on a new roof," said Mom.

"The last one got smashed. A space rock hit it."

"Here is our new house now!" called Dad.

I could see the house as we landed.

It was yellow and silver. We landed right on the roof.

Then, we slid down into the house.

page 5

"I will put away the food," said Mom.

"I will help!" I said.

"I will put water dust in the well," said Dad.

- -

page 6

The next day, I went to school.

No one told me that I had to wear heavy shoes to school.

I floated in the air all day. I had to do math as I floated.

I had to write spelling words as I floated.

I even had to paint as I floated!

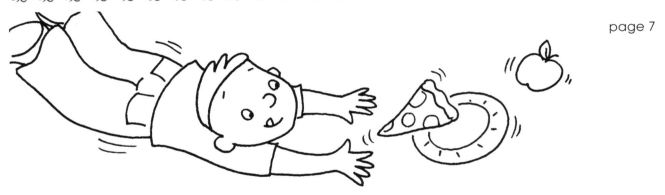

But, I had fun. My new teacher gave me help.
I got to eat lunch in the air.
My pizza floated in front of me!
A bell rang at the end of the day.
I went to the jet pad. I flew home.
People waved as I flew by.

"Now, how was school?" asked Mom.
"Did you have fun? Did you like it?"
"Well, life on IK2B3 is not like our old home," I said.
"But, I think it went very well. I think I will like it here!"
Mom smiled.
"Mom," I said. "Can we go buy some new shoes?"

Name _____

Name _____

Letter Maze

Circle the letters that spell "**help**."

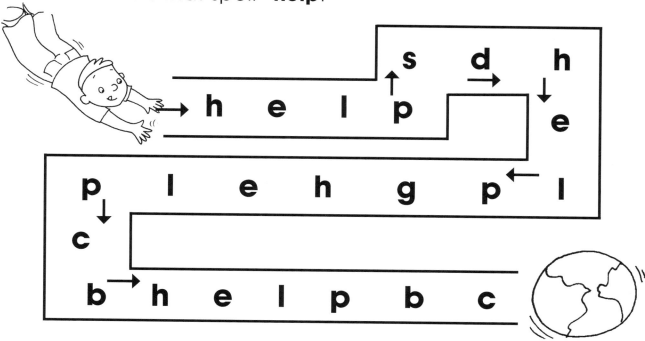

Pyramid Words

Build a pyramid for the word "**very**."

1. __V_____

2. _____ _____

3. _____ _____ _____

4. _____ _____ _____ _____

Name _____

Coloring Words

Color all of the spaceships that have the word "**these**."

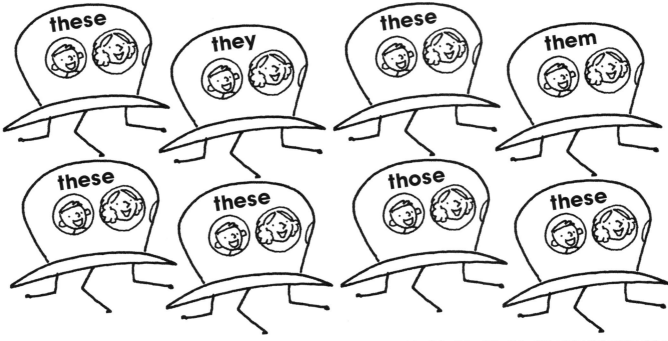

Finish the Sentence

Write the word "**new**" or "**now**" to finish each sentence.

1. _____, I have some homework to do.

2. I go to a _____ school.

3. Did you get some _____ shoes?

4. What should we do _____?

Our New Home: Flannel Board Patterns

Directions: Use these patterns to make flannel-board storytelling pieces for the story on pages 105–108. Copy the patterns onto card stock, color them, cut them out, and laminate them for durability. Finally, glue sandpaper or place self-stick hook-and-loop tape on the back of each piece.

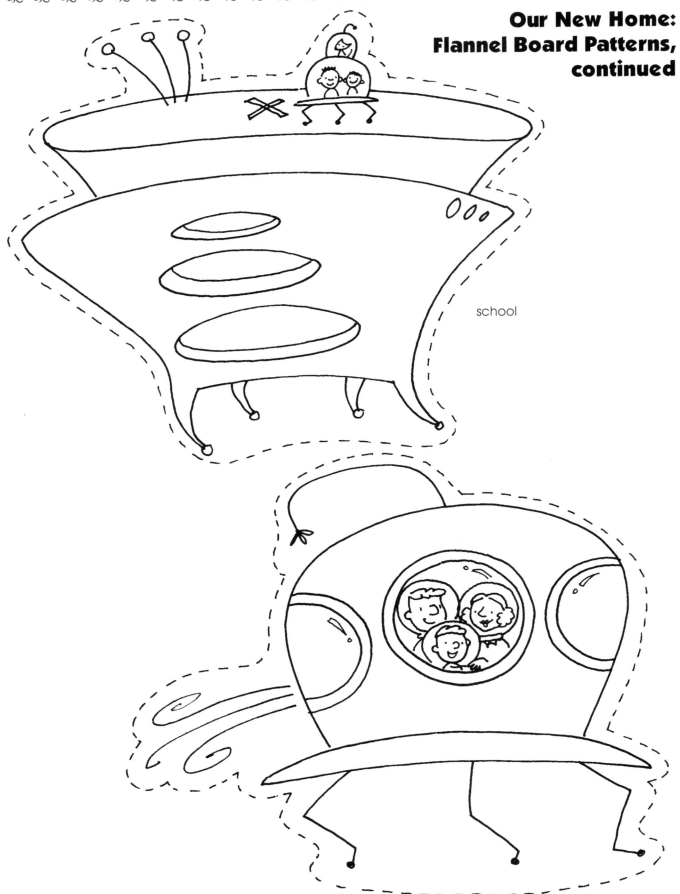

school

Our New Home: Flannel Board Patterns, continued

home

Poem Title:

Change

Sight Words Included:

girl

got

stop

what

where

which

Looking at Sight Words

1. Make copies of the poem (page 116). Ask students to find and circle the following sight words that are featured in this poem: *girl*, *got*, *stop*, *what*, *where*, *which*.

2. Model writing the individual letters of each sight word on the board. Then, ask students to practice writing the words.

3. Look for other sight words in the poem that have already been introduced in previous stories and poems: *and*, *big*, *boy*, *look*. You can also work with students on these words. See the Table of Contents on pages 3 and 4 to find in which story or poem each word is featured.

Playing with Sight Words

1. Play the "Let's Change This Word!" game. Ask students what words they could make if they changed the first letters or sound in *stop*. What if they changed the first sound in *where*? What words could students make by changing the /g/ in *got* to a different sound? Be sure to write each sight word on the board as you play so that students see and read the original word and gain familiarity with it.

2. Copy pages 117 and 118 for each student. Have students complete the pages and color the pictures.

3. Make copies of page 119. Have students work in groups or individually to complete the exercise and then color the pictures. Review the sight words in the activity after students have finished working.

Follow-Up Activities

1. Present a science unit about changes in the natural world: caterpillars into butterflies, seeds into plants, seasonal changes, etc.

2. Talk about changes students see in their own lives. How have their families changed since they were younger? How has going to school changed their lives? What changes do they like? Which ones do they find difficult?

Change

Stop and look!

Every girl and boy

Grows to be big and tall.

The trees of green

got leaves of gold

As summer turned to fall.

The baby bird,

Which hopped along,

Is now flying free.

And, where there was

A cold, bare hill,

There are flowers and bees.

Stop and look!

You will see

Things that are brand new.

What was here keeps changing,

And you are changing, too!

Tic-Tac-Toe

Circle the letters that spell "**got**."

f	a	t
t	o	o
g	o	t

Letter Maze

Circle the letters that spell "**what**."

w h v a t c w m h f a t

Name _____

Missing Letters

Fill in the missing letters to write "**which**" or "**where**."

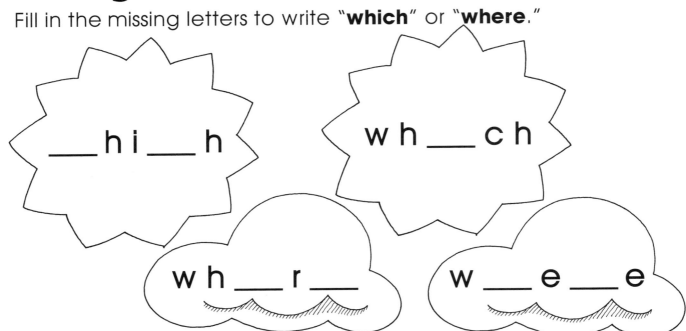

_ h i _ _ h

w h _ _ c h

w h _ _ r _ _

w _ _ e _ _ e

Coloring Words

Color all of the signs that have the word "**stop**."

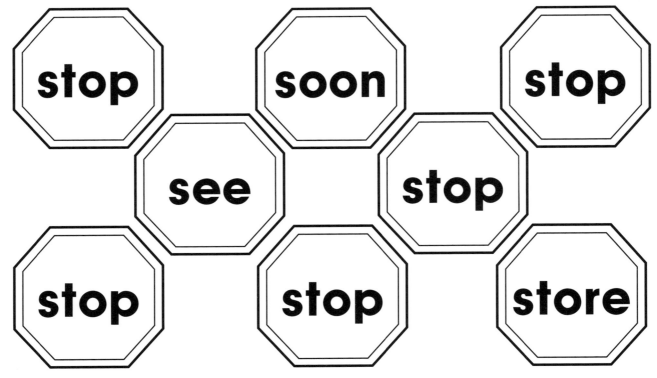

stop   soon   stop

see   stop

stop   stop   store

Name _____

Change: Activity Page

Directions: Color the picture that matches the sentence.

This is a girl.

The mouse runs.

The bees are in the flowers.

The boy is tall.

Story Title: # Snails See the Sea

ℰG •ℰG •ℰG •ℰG •ℰG •ℰG •ℰG •ℰG •ℰG •ℰG •ℰG •ℰG •ℰG •ℰG •ℰG •ℰG •ℰG •ℰG •ℰG •ℰG •ℰG •ℰG •

Sight Words Included:

been

her

let

than

us

use

work

Looking at Sight Words

1. Make copies of the story (pages 121–124). Cut each page apart along the dashed line, assemble the story's pages in order, and staple it along the left edge. Ask students to find and circle all of the following sight words that are featured in this story: *been*, *her*, *let*, *than*, *us*, *use*, *work*.

2. Explain to students the difference between *sea* and *see* in the story. Use this as an introduction to other homophones, for example, *be* and *bee* in the poem "A Friend for Bear" on pages 52 and 53. Other sight word homophones include *ate/eight*, *for/four*, and *to/too/two*.

3. Look for other sight words in the story that have already been introduced: *funny*, *get*, *go*, *had*, *is*, *on*, *said*, *was*, *we*. You can also work with students on these words. See the Table of Contents on pages 3 and 4 to find in which story or poem each word is featured.

Playing with Sight Words

1. Make alphabet letter cards to spell each of the featured sight words. Create a set for each group of students. Have students work in teams to assemble the featured sight words with the cards.

2. Copy pages 125 and 126 for each student. Have students complete the pages and color the pictures.

3. Make copies of page 127. Ask students to solve the maze and then color the pictures. They can work in groups or teams for this activity.

Follow-Up Activities

1. Study snails! Consider setting up or borrowing an aquarium with a snail habitat. Have students observe the snails—particularly their travel speed.

2. Talk about what life would be like if everyone moved very slowly. How long would it take to fix dinner? How would slow traffic change our world? Have students draw pictures of this "slow world" view.

Snails See the Sea

Sue Snail had been to the beach.
She had seen the sea.
It had taken her two years to get there.
"No one moves slower than we do," she said sadly.

"Maybe we can use another way to go home,"
said Sally Snail.
Sally was Sue's friend.

Sue said, "Would a bird carry us home?"
"A bird may eat us," said Sally.

page 4

"Could we go in a car?" asked Sue.
"Who would let us drive?" said Sally. "We are snails."

"We could work.
Then, we could buy tickets to go on a bus," said Sue.

"That is funny. What job could a snail do?" asked Sally.
Sue nodded. She hung her head. Sally was right.
What could they do?

page 7

Sally looked around.
"It is very nice here. It is nicer than home," she said.
"That is it!" cried Sue.

page 8

Sally and Sue built a new home. It was at the beach.
That way, they did not have to make the trip again.
They were very happy.

Tic-Tac-Toe

Circle the letters that spell "**let**."

t	l	l
h	e	n
f	t	t

Coloring Words

Color the pictures that have the word "**us**" or "**use**."

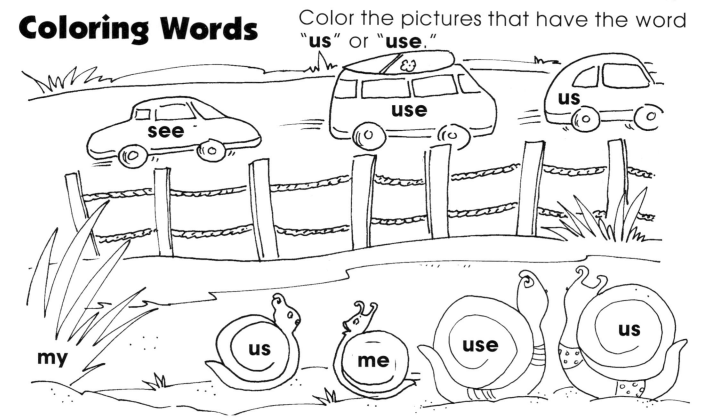

Missing Letters

Fill in the missing letters to write "**work**."

__ __ o r __ __

w __ __ k

__ __ __ r k

w o __ __ __

Word Search

Circle the words "**her**."

h	h	e	r
z	e	y	h
a	r	r	e
a	h	e	r

Name _____

Snails See the Sea: Activity Page

Directions: Help Sally and Sue go to the beach. Circle the words in the **word bank** to get to the beach.

been	her	let	than	us	use	work

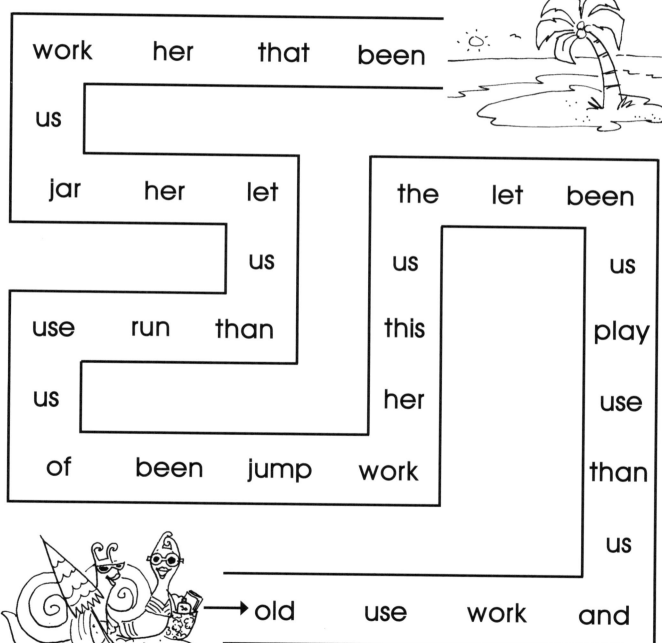

Extra Practice Stories and Poems

The following pages include both stories and poems that feature some of the 170 sight words introduced in this book. For activities related to these words, see the original units where the words were introduced. See the Table of Contents on pages 3 and 4 in which story or poem each word is featured or use one of the general activities or games below:

1. **Sound Out the Sight Words**
   Sound out the sight words. Ask students to repeat the separate sounds and then combine the sounds to say the complete word.

2. **Write the Sight Words**
   Write the sight words from the story or poem on a board or on cards. Ask students to read the sight words to you. You can divide the class into teams and turn this reading activity into a game or even a relay race.

3. **Sight Word Word Wall**
   Create a word wall for the sight words from each story and poem. Be sure to include daily practice sessions to help students strengthen their recognition of these words.

4. **Word Families**
   Take the onset off of individual sight words and then create word families for each word. Write the original sight word at the top of each word family list to show each list's "parent" word.

5. **Brainstorm Word Lists**
   Ask students to brainstorm lists of words that rhyme with each sight word. Or, read pairs of words and ask students to raise their hands if the two words rhyme.

6. **Circle Sight Words**
   Make copies of each story or poem. Ask students to circle the featured sight words and then underline all of the other sight words with which they've worked. Using the sight word wall for reference, challenge students to find as many sight words as possible in each reading selection.

Sick Day

page 1

I had to stay home from school. I was sick.
My nose was red. My eyes hurt. I felt hot.
I did not want to see TV. I did not want to sleep.
I did not want to read. I did not want to paint.

- -

page 2

So, what did I do? I sang!
I sang all of the songs I knew.
Then, I made up some songs. I sang about my dog.
I sang about my mom. I sang about my house.
I sang about soup. I sang about my new ball.

At first, my songs were soft. Then, I sang loudly.
It made me feel good. I smiled.
Then, it was time for dinner. Mom made me soup.
She had made me cookies. I felt good!

The next day, my teacher said, "How are you?"
"I feel fine," I said. "I want to be a singer when I grow up.
Or a doctor. Or a singing doctor!"

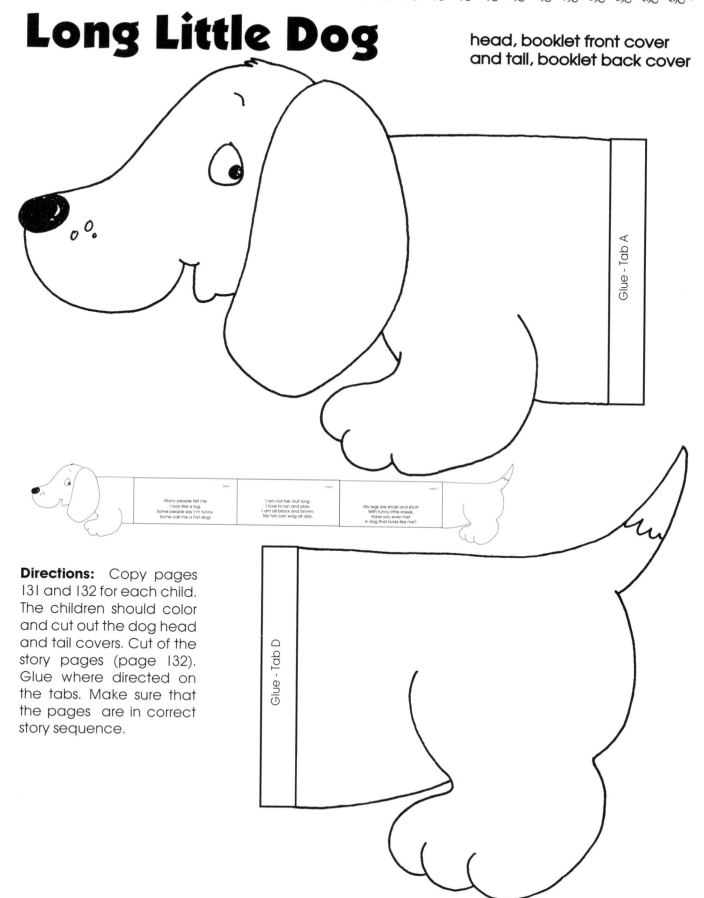

Long Little Dog

head, booklet front cover
and tail, booklet back cover

Glue - Tab A

Glue - Tab D

Many people tell me
I look like a log.
Some people say I'm funny.
Some call me a hot dog!

I am not tall, but long.
I love to run and play.
I am all black and brown.
My tail can wag all day.

My legs are small and short
With funny little knees.
Have you ever met
A dog that looks like me?

Directions: Copy pages 131 and 132 for each child. The children should color and cut out the dog head and tail covers. Cut of the story pages (page 132). Glue where directed on the tabs. Make sure that the pages are in correct story sequence.

page 1

Glue - Tab A

Glue - Tab B

Many people tell me
I look like a log.
Some people say I'm funny.
Some call me a hot dog!

page 2

Glue - Tab B

Glue - Tab B

I am not tall, but long.
I love to run and play.
I am all black and brown.
My tail can wag all day.

page 3

Glue - Tab B

Glue - Tab D

My legs are small and short
With funny little knees.
Have you ever met
A dog that looks like me?

The Trip

It was time to go on our car trip.
We were going to see my aunt.
It was going to be a long ride.
My mom and dad packed the car.
We had clothes. We had snacks. We had maps.
We took our dog, Buffy. We took our cat, Fluffy.

We started to drive. The baby slept.
Mom played games with me. We played "I Spy."
We looked for all the red cars. We counted things.
I read a book. I ate an orange. I kicked the seat.
"Are we there yet?" I asked.
"Not yet," said Dad.

Then, Fluffy climbed over Buffy. Buffy barked.
The baby woke up. Buffy licked her face.
The baby cried. Fluffy climbed on the baby.
The baby cried again.
"Time for a break," said Dad.

We sat under a tree. We ate hot dogs.
Mom got the baby back to sleep.
Then, we started to drive again.
We drove and drove. I read another book.
Mom and I counted all the yellow cars.

Then, Buffy saw a cow. She barked.
The baby woke up. She cried.
Fluffy hid under the seat. She hissed.
"Time for a break," said Mom.

page 6

This time, we got ice cream.
We walked in a little park.
Then, we got back in the car.
"Are we almost there?" I asked.
"Almost," said Mom.

Buffy and Fluffy started to fight. I held Buffy.
Mom held Fluffy. Dad said, "Are we there yet?"
"Yes!" said Mom. She smiled. "There is Aunt Jill's house."

"Yay!" I called out.
"Thank goodness," said Dad.
Buffy barked. Fluffy purred. The baby clapped her hands.
The trip was over!

The Dream

Go up the stairs.
Go down the hall.
Go into the room
That has no wall.

page 3

page 4

Jump into the boat
That is waiting there.
Go under the bridge
To the funny fair

Where animals talk
And people sing
And clowns do tricks
And everything

It's bright and white
And full of noise.
There all the dreaming
Girls and boys

Can stay and play
Before their boats
Turn into beds
And night is day.

Berry Time

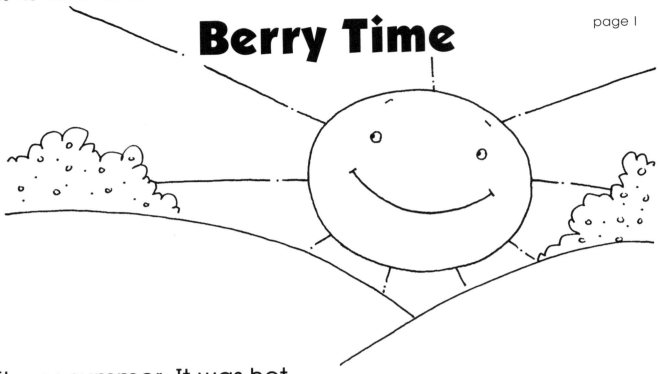

It was summer. It was hot.
The sun was big and yellow in the blue sky.

"Guess what?" Aunt Jill asked.
"What?" I said.
"Today we are going to pick berries," she said.

I live in the city. We have parks. We have grass.
We even have a little lake. But, we do not have berries.
"And here, I get to go and pick them?" I asked.
"Yes," said Aunt Jill.

page 3

page 4

We took hats. We took pails.
We hiked to the place where the berries grew.
"You can start here," said Aunt Jill. "I will go over there."

It was hot. The berries were little. I stepped on some.

I dropped some. But, I got some in my pail.

"How are you?" Aunt Jill called.

"OK," I said. But, I was not OK. I was very hot.

I was very cross.

And, I got my shirt hooked on some thorns.

---

page 6

I pulled. I pulled hard. I could not get free.

I felt like a big dog was biting me.

I dropped my pail. All of my berries fell on the ground.

"HELP!" I cried. Aunt Jill ran to me. She got my shirt free.

She picked up my pail.
"It is OK," she said. "I have lots of berries."
We went back home.
Aunt Jill gave me a glass of cold water.

Then, she made a pie. It was full of berries.
I ate some pie. "How is it?" she asked.
"It is good," I said. "It is berry good!"

Vacation Plans

Go for ice cream,
Meet a friend,
Sit on a rock
Around the bend.
Buy a book,
Dance in the yard,

Sing a song,
Choose a card.
Swim at the pool,
Lie on the lawn,
Watch the stars,
And wake at dawn.

Sugar and Spice

page 1

One day, two little mice went to look for cheese.
One was named Sugar. One was named Spice.
"I saw some cheese in the farmer's house," said Sugar.

page 2

"It is not safe," said Spice. "The farmer has two cats."
"I can take care of them," said Sugar.
Sugar went to the barn. She got some hay.
She put it on the steps to the house.

Three cows came out of the barn.
They started to eat the hay.
The farmer's wife opened the door.
She called to the cows, "Go away!"

The two cats ran out of the house.
The two little mice ran in.
"Good work," said Spice.
"Thank you," said Sugar.
"Now, we need to look for the cheese."

They went into the kitchen.
"There it is!" said Spice. "But, it is up too high."
"I can take care of that," said Sugar.

- -

She ran up a chair. She jumped onto the counter.
She ran to a rolling pin. Sugar pushed and pushed.
The pin rolled. It hit the cheese. The cheese fell down.

page 7

Sugar and Spice ate and ate.
They grew fat and full and round.
Then, the farmer came in.
"Hey!" he cried. "There are mice in here!"

page 8

"Run, Spice!" yelled Sugar.
Spice tried to run.
He was so full and so fat that he could not run.

"Roll, Spice!" yelled Sugar.
Spice fell down. He rolled like a ball.
Sugar ran out the door. Spice rolled out the door.

The two mice hid. "That was close," said Sugar.
"But, that cheese was so good!"
"I will not walk for a week," said poor Spice.
And, he did not.

Two Squirrels

If I run up the hill,

Will you run, too?

Will you chase me

If I chase you?

If I find your food,

Will you dig up mine?

If I steal eight nuts,

Will you take nine?

If I build a nest

High up in this tree,

Will you build one, too,

And come to see me?

Lost!

Chen went shopping with his Mom.
They had many things to buy.
"We need rice," said Mom.
So, they went to the rice seller. They got a big bag of rice.

"We need fish," said Mom.
They went to look at all of the fish.
The fish were set out on big trays of ice.
Mom bought four fish.
"Now, we need snow peas," said Mom.
She went to the man who had vegetables.

Chen started to go, too. But then, he saw the puppet.
It was a dragon. A man was making the dragon dance.
It was funny. Lots of kids stood and watched.
Chen stood and looked at the dragon.
Then, he looked up. He did not see Mom. Mom was gone!
"Mom!" he called. He ran.

Chen went to the vegetable seller.
"Have you seen my Mom?" he asked.
"Who is your Mom?" the seller asked.
Chen did not know what to say. Mom was Mom.
He just shook his head. Then, he ran again.

Chen ran to the fish seller.
"Have you seen my Mom?" he asked.
"She was just here with you," said the seller. "But, she left."

Chen ran to the rice seller.
"Have you seen my Mom?" he asked.
"What is her name?" the rice seller asked.
"Mom," said Chen.

Chen walked back to the man with the puppet.
The dragon did not seem so funny.
Then, Chen looked up. Mom was there!

Mom smiled. "I saw you stop here," she said.
"But, when I came back, I did not see you.
You must stay with me, Chen."
Chen hugged his Mom. "I will from now on!" he said.

Party Dress

"Watch your little sister," Dad said to me.
He went down the stairs. Then, he called up to me.
"Help her pick out a dress for the party."

"Did you hear that?" I asked.
"Can you pick out a party dress?"
She nodded. She pointed.

page 3

"That one?" I asked.
It was her costume from Halloween.
She had been a queen.
"That is not a dress for a real party," I said.

- -

page 4

She looked at me. Her face got red.
I knew she was about to cry. "OK, OK!" I said.
"You can wear that."
I helped her put on the shiny blue dress.

"What shoes do you want to wear?" I asked.

She pointed at her snow boots.

"These are not party shoes," I said.

She looked at me. She shut her eyes.

She opened her mouth.

I knew she was about to scream.

"OK!" I said. "You can wear them."

I helped her put on the boots. She pointed again.

She pointed at her big beach hat.

"You do not need a hat at a party," I said.

She looked at me.

I did not wait to see if she would cry or scream.

"OK, you can wear that," I said.

She put on the big hat.

She put on a big string of beads.
She put on a ring with a big red stone.
She put a purple clip in her hair.
Then, she put a pair of socks on her hands.
"You look great," I said.

Dad called up.
"It is time for the party!" he said. "Are you two ready?"
"Yes," I called back.
"I hope you are ready for the best party dress ever!"

Anything

If you could have anything,
What would you get?
An elephant? Moon rocks?
The world's biggest train set?

- -

If you could be anything,
What would you be?
A rock star? A painter?
A sailor at sea?

If you could do anything,
What would you do?
Fly a rocket? Find new lands?
Run a store or a zoo?